Getting Retail Right!

Getting Retail Right!

Improving Productivity with the Right Communication, Training, Merchandising, Marketing, and Tenant-Mix/Leasing Strategies

John C. Williams

 International Council of Shopping Centers

About The International Council of Shopping Centers

The International Council of Shopping Centers (ICSC) is the trade association of the shopping center industry. Serving the shopping center industry since 1957, ICSC is a not-for-profit organization with over 46,000 members in 77 countries worldwide.

ICSC members include shopping center

- owners
- developers
- managers
- marketing specialists
- leasing agents
- retailers
- researchers
- attorneys

- architects
- contractors
- consultants
- investors
- lenders and brokers
- academics
- public officials

ICSC holds more than 200 meetings a year throughout the world and provides a wide array of services and products for shopping center professionals, including deal making events, conferences, educational programs, accreditation, awards, publications and research data.

For more information about ICSC, write or call:
The International Council of Shopping Centers
1221 Avenue of the Americas, 41st Floor
New York, NY 10020-1099
Telephone: 646.728.3800
Fax: 212.589.5555
info@icsc.org
http://www.icsc.org

This publication is designed to provide accurate and authoritative information in regard to the subject matter covered. It is sold with the understanding that the publisher is not engaged in rendering legal, accounting, or other professional services. If legal advice or other expert assistance is required, the services of a competent professional person should be sought.
—From a Declaration of Principles jointly adopted
by a Committee of the American Bar Association
and a Committee of Publishers.

Companies, professional groups, clubs and other organizations may qualify for special terms when ordering quantities of more than 20 of this title.

INTERNATIONAL COUNCIL OF SHOPPING CENTERS
Publications Department
1221 Avenue of the Americas
New York, NY 10020-1099

BOOK DESIGN: Harish Patel Design
COVER DESIGN: DK&G Creative Services

ICSC Catalog Number: 234

International Standard Book Number: 1-58268-040-X

Contents

Acknowledgments

No book is the result of just one person's efforts. In this case, I would like to thank Cheryl Desormeaux from J.C. Williams Group, who went through seven drafts; Jay Kahane capably prepared the section on retail IT and business processes; Megan Williams played the role of editor and coach; and, of course, there are too many friends in the shopping center industry to mention, who listened to the ideas and who contributed their wealth of experience and knowledge. Also, the team at ICSC, led by Patricia Montagni, Director of Publications, was very supportive throughout the whole process.

— J.C.W.

ICSC gratefully acknowledges Christine Menna, Pennsylvania State University, and Craig B. Sorrels, CSWG, Inc., for their time and expertise in reviewing this publication.

Introduction

Shopping and retailing have never been more complex. Where once they were limited in time, with regular hours and days in which stores were closed, they're now 24/7. Where they were once linked to place — town or shopping centers — they're now everywhere. From the proliferation of e-retailing as an adjunct to catalogs to shopping in airplanes, call-in or call-out centers, entertainment events or venues, retailing is ubiquitous, wide-open and ever-transforming.

This is exciting. Constrictions and traditional boundaries fall by the wayside and an endless opportunity for creative innovation is present in a way it has never been in the past. And along with the technology, consumers are driving the change. Expectations are higher than they've ever been. People want wider assortments that are cheaper, better, everywhere, and most of all *now*.

Subsequently, the shopping center professionals' job is the most demanding it's ever been. It requires vision, creativity, an understanding of psychology, sociology, economics, not to mention technology and simply quick wits.

Getting Retail Right! is written with a simple objective: to help shopping center management and retailers improve their productivity. Retail isn't easy, but by understanding the various forces and options that need to be considered when making key decisions, success can be achieved.

This book will help you tune in to your center's retail world. You'll learn about how to showcase rising stars, improve the middle performers, and spot stores that are in trouble. You'll read about merchandising and customer services, financial planning, design and layout, visual presentation, and the role of information technology and business support. You'll learn about getting the tenant mix right.

Getting Retail Right! is written specifically with shopping center management in mind and some chapters speak directly to the center manager, although even senior management should find new ideas here. And retailers, too, can benefit directly from the wealth of advice and instruction at the store level while gaining insight into management's expectations and responsibilities. In addition, center leasing and tenant coordination professionals, who may find the book a practical-knowledge builder and reference guide, and support services people, such as shopping center designers, marketers, advertising executives, and special events organizers, can pick up valuable information, ideas, and tips.

Getting Retail Right! is organized into ten chapters covering the following major topics:

- **Understanding retailers and identifying weaknesses (Chapters 1 and 2)**
- **Working with retailers (Chapter 3)**
- **Ways to increase retailer productivity (Chapter 4 – 7)**
- **Dealing with operations and rent issues (Chapter 8, 9)**
- **New approaches to tenant mix (Chapter 10)**

Despite the turmoil of the retail world, the goal of both retail and shopping center management is to be financially successful by serving the shopper better than anyone else. This goal can only be met if each "player" has the best understanding possible of how the other players function. In a win-win game, shopping center management will help to ensure that retail tenants are in top form and productive. And retailers will be able to come to management for strategic advice. In this mutually dependent industry, developers and retailers play with two very different strategic approaches: the developer plays a long-term game of land acquisition and massive capital investment for asset appreciation and consistent cash flow; the retailer plays with a short-term operational focus and needs relatively low capital investment. However, both serve the same consumer and need to work as one. We wish you success in this – in winning all your games and keeping your fans, the customers, happy.

1. Understanding Retailing

Characteristics of Successful Retailers

One of the fascinating things about retailing is that while there are just a handful of basic principals for success, there are thousands of ways to implement each principal. Think, for example, of the store that specializes exceptionally well in one category of merchandise to great success (e.g., Bombay Company, Williams-Sonoma, American Girl, Talbots, and Lands' End). This has been done hundreds of different ways. Yet in each case, the following key characteristics are generally present.

Successful Retailers Are Customer Focused

Whether a Wal-Mart or a great "Mom and Pop," retailers who thrive are devoted to their target market customer segment. Either through extensive market research, or by being alert "on the floor," the winners are continually listening, watching, and testing new ideas to serve and delight shoppers. This approach can range from price rollbacks, to introducing exotic merchandise, to offering new services. While none of these concepts are new, a successful store must have a clear definition of who its target market segment is and is not. In other words, successful retailers are highly focused. They zoom in on one important segment and understand it thoroughly. Whether high-end like Gucci, Nieman Marcus and Tiffany & Co; or lower-end like Dollar General or Fred's; or traditional like Ralph Lauren, Talbot's, and Lands' End; or avant-garde like Betsy Johnson, French Connection, or Design Within Reach, these stores understand the needs, wants, and whims of their core customers. Market knowledge drives their strategy. Winning retailers understand that being all things to all people is a recipe for disaster.

Use the following Four Es Retail Solutions Strategy Model as a way
of thinking about having a customer-focused strategy. There are four
main consumer shopping needs:

- saving time,

- saving money,

- having an enjoyable experience, and

- supporting ego needs.

We suggest that retailers choose one (or two at the most) to focus
their resources. Of course a store has to be good at all of these, but
to succeed it must excel at one. This can only be done by channeling
all resources on the type of shopper that is primarily motivated by
efficiency, economy, entertainment, or ego.

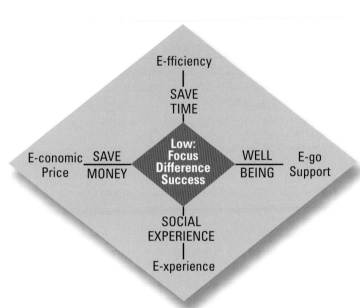

Source: J.C. Williams Group

Stores that do not have a clear strategic focus and that gravitate
towards a central position on this chart become undifferentiated and
usually fail.

Four Es Retail Solutions Strategy Model:

Characteristics of Each Solution

E-fficiency

- Handy location, hours of operation
- Layout, signage, checkout
- Catalogue – e-retail support
- Assortment dominance
- Convenience stores or big box or e-retail

- Culture: Save the shopper time
- IT: Multi-channel, assortment management, service efficiency, CRM
- Marketing: Brand recognition
- Product: Quick to-go, prepared

E-conomy

- Operational efficiency
- Supply chain management
- Lowest prices
- Wal-mart, Price Costco, Payless ShoeSource

- Culture: Save money, pass on to the shopper
- IT: effective speed, in-stock, high turnover, low investment
- Marketing: move product
- Product: good quality at lowest price

E-go

- Status
- Quality beyond physical experience
- New (private) brand structure
- Neiman Marcus. BMW, Tiffany

- Culture: Attuned to the consumer segment
- IT: Creative process, CRM
- Marketing: Create emotional value
- Product: Badge value and status

E-xperience
E-ducation, E-ntertainment,
E-nvironment

- Learning, free fun, sensual, sophisticated
- Constant renewal
- Barnes & Noble, amazon.com, Hard Rock Café

- Culture: Creative
- IT: Flexibility, information, basics
- Marketing: Part of the experience
- Product: Exotic, organic, ethnic

Successful Retailers Are High-Energy People

Running a store is a complex, demanding business. There is enormous pressure to please shoppers. If that weren't already enough, attracting, training, and motivating staff is never-ending, especially in an industry that isn't known for its high pay at entry and junior levels. In addition, there are relationships with suppliers, delivery firms, financial institutions, landlords, marketing agencies, and technology services. All this takes place in an industry that is open long hours and run primarily on the labor of part-time, fairly low-paid staff. That staff also has to be scheduled to cover peak times, as well as evenings and weekends. There must be time for systems, selling skills, and product knowledge training; plus the operational activities of selling, layaways, and special orders.

In addition to serving customers, sales associates have to stock shelves, plus perform a myriad of other duties.

Within the store there is a constant juggling of activity beyond dealing with people. New merchandise has to be put out in the store, advertised items must be featured, shelves stocked, slow-selling items marked down, faulty items returned, window displays constructed, floors cleaned, all types of money transactions accounted for, and customer web-based purchases picked up or returned. In short, retailing is tough and demanding and requires stamina.

Successful Retailers Are Skilled Managers

If dealing confidently and fairly with people doesn't come naturally, it's time to focus on ways to improve people skills. Successful retailers distinguish themselves by the way they deal with their team and their customers. Customer devotion is shown in hundreds of ways, from a clean store, full inventory on shelves or racks to an enthusiastic staff. These are some of the outward signs. Yet just as important are the inner, behind-the-scenes workings such as use of information technology (IT) and business processes that make it easier to be customer-focused.

Retailers cannot serve customers competitively without IT and business processes that will support their strategy. If the strategy is economy-focused (like Wal-Mart or Family Dollar), the business process will support efficient materials-handling logistics, reporting product sales to suppliers, paperless payment to suppliers, and collaborative planning and forecasting. All of this helps to drive costs down that can be passed on as savings to the consumers.

An efficiency strategy means ensuring that your target-market shopper's trip is as hassle-free as possible. This can be done by:

- offering a full-service approach (i.e., we-do-it-all-for-you) that involves a motivated, fully trained staff who is supported by technology such as, customer relationship management strategies (CRM), which is database tracking of shoppers' purchase patterns that responds to the customer's needs in advance of their requests.

Computers open a world of assortments, plus track customer purchase patterns.

This requires software programs to manage the basic customer information and track shopping patterns (i.e., the frequency, type of purchase, and dollar amount over time) so that you can quickly anticipate shopping and service needs. Never underestimate the loyalty of a well-served customer and the benefits that can bring a store. By figuring out who the best customers are and understanding that by giving them highly personal service, this will reinforce their loyalty. Supporting these special customers means focusing on their needs, gearing merchandise assortments to them, engaging in one-to-one marketing communications, and offering them special services.

Just as efficient is the one-stop shop. This type of retailer tends to have huge assortments of goods in large spaces. Shoppers are more willing to drive the extra distance to go to Home Depot or Toys "R" Us, for example, than to drop in at various retailers in an attempt to find what they want. One-stop stores are typically semi-self-service with superior product information, a range of support services, and competitive pricing.

Self-service can be an efficient experience if it is well-organized.

Successful Retailers Embrace Positive Competitiveness

It goes without saying that winning stores are industry leaders. These are retailers that outshine the others, that dazzle as "shopper pleasers." Winning stores take their cues both from what the competition is up to as well as innovations in other industry sectors. But much of what fires their success is what they learn from listening to and observing consumers. By casting light on two sources – the standards set by competitors and what shoppers are saying – they soar.

Positive competitiveness strategic decisions are based on moving store performance from:

Adequate performance Trying to meet shopper's needs	=	Shopper acceptance High turnover No loyalty

⬇

Above standard performance that differentiates from competition	=	Shopper preference On their retail short-list

⬇

Exceptional performance Dominating the market Leader in shopper's mind	=	Start shopping trip Loyal, low turnover An apostle

Here are different levels of commitment that affect how a shopper moves through a retail experience:

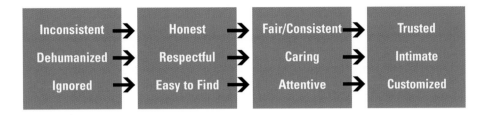

In other words, go from good, to great, to spectacular. The highest level always brings out the "WOW!" – as in a customer exclaiming, "WOW! I will definitely come back here, and tell friends about it, too!"

Successful Retailers Are Creative

While many people are attracted to the business of retail for the creativity involved—the chance to shape and build a world of their own (their store!)—this creativity can often get lost in the shuffle of the daily routine. When this happens it is time to shift gears and start thinking about retailing not as merely an outlet that sells things to the public, but as entertaining, educational, and transforming. Think of The Disney Store, Barnes and Noble, and Hard Rock Café, for example. But creativity goes further. Shoppers expect retailers to give them a taste of the future. Retailers can respond to that desire by leading in merchandise categories the way Loblaw Group's "President's Choice" grocery products and Target have done. Other examples include new store designs like Apple computers; or by offering special services the way Nordstrom's concierge desk and Amazon.com did; by lowering prices like the warehouse clubs or Payless Shoe Source, and, of course, American Girl and Build-A-Bear Workshop have created entirely new retail concepts!

How Retailing Works

The role of retailing in the consumer "value chain" is simple: with the exception of those retailers who create and make their own products, retailing does not create or manufacture. Within the value chain, retailing adds "time and place" value for the consumer. The diagram below illustrates this:

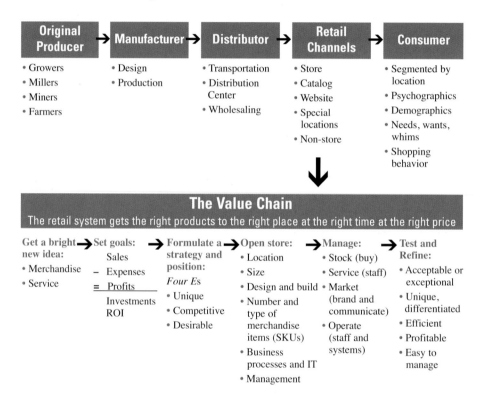

Original Producer	→	Manufacturer	→	Distributor	→	Retail Channels	→	Consumer
• Growers • Millers • Miners • Farmers		• Design • Production		• Transportation • Distribution Center • Wholesaling		• Store • Catalog • Website • Special locations • Non-store		• Segmented by location • Psychographics • Demographics • Needs, wants, whims • Shopping behavior

The Value Chain

The retail system gets the right products to the right place at the right time at the right price

| Get a bright new idea:
• Merchandise
• Service | → | Set goals:
   Sales
– Expenses
= Profits
   Investments
   ROI | → | Formulate a strategy and position:
Four Es
• Unique
• Competitive
• Desirable | → | Open store:
• Location
• Size
• Design and build
• Number and type of merchandise items (SKUs)
• Business processes and IT
• Management | → | Manage:
• Stock (buy)
• Service (staff)
• Market (brand and communicate)
• Operate (staff and systems) | → | Test and Refine:
• Acceptable or exceptional
• Unique, differentiated
• Efficient
• Profitable
• Easy to manage |

Retail Financial Model

Understanding a retailer profit and loss or operating statement is a straightforward task. In a nutshell, the store buys merchandise at one price and sells it at a higher price with enough left over to pay expenses and enjoy a profit. Most retailers (except the food industry) use the "retail inventory method" of accounting, which means that the inventory is tracked or accounted for at the retail selling price, *not* the wholesale price. All measurements are on the net selling price ("sales"). Keep in mind that these are industry "typical" and that a line item metric can vary 25–50% for any given retailer.

Retail Operating Statement: Shopping Center-Based Store

Typical Operating or Profit and Loss Statement (year, $ 000)		Apparel		Electronics		Fast Food	
	Comment	$	%	$	%	$	%
a. Sales	Net of returns, taxes	$1,000	100%	$2,000	100%	$600	100%
b. Less cost of goods	Manufacturer's price and freight	$-500	-50%	$-1,400	-70%	$-180	-30%
c. Less markdowns, shrinkage	Workrooms, theft, price reductions	$-100	-15%	$-200	-10%	$-30	-5%
d. Gross margin	a-(b+c) = d	$400	40%	$400	20%	$390	65%
e. In-store expenses							
f. Wages and benefits	Managers and staff	$120	12%	$120	6%	$120	20%
g. Occupancy • Rent	Rent, rent %, and CAM, taxes	$100	9%	$100	5%	$60	10%
• Other		$30	3%	$20	1%	$60	10%
h. Marketing	All related	$10	1%	$10	.5%	$20	3%
i. Office and misc.	Suppliers and telecom	$20	2%	$10	.5%	$10	1%
j. Total	All in-store expenses	$280	28%	$260	13%	$270	45%
k. Store contribution to company profit	d – j = k	$120	12%	$140	7%	$120	20%
l. Less non-store expenses • Management	Home office	$5	.5%	$10	.5%	$10	1.7%
• Accounting	MIS, IT, CRM	$10	1%	$10	.5%	$10	1.7%
• Materials handling	Trucks, DC	$5	.5%	$10	.5%	$10	1.8%
• Financial	Banks, credit	$10	1%	$10	.5%	$10	1.8%
• Marketing	"National" program	$20	2%	$20	1%	$20	3%
m. Total non-store expenses	**All of the above**	**$50**	**5%**	**$60**	**3%**	**$60**	**10%**
n. Earnings before depreciation, interest/interest	k – m = n	$70	7%	$80	4%	$60	10%
o. Taxes/Interest		$20	2%	$10	.5%	$20	3%
p. Net income	n – o = p	$50	5%	$70	3.5%	$40	8%

Source: Various trade association reports, company annual reports, and proprietary information of J.C. Williams Group.

This profit and loss statement gives you a snapshot of the store's operations on a to-date and periodic (usually monthly) basis. Please keep in mind that (a) these figures are general and any store can out-or underperform, (b) that lines A to K are meant to show in-center operations, while lines L to P are home/regional office operations.

Key Performance Indicators (KPI)

One of the fascinating opportunities for center management is to observe the various levels of performance for similar stores. The key issue is, why do stores selling the same commodity vary so much in performance? The answer to this question is what this book is about. Most shopping centers report tenant performance by commodity or category, which facilitates direct comparison of similar store sales and productivity metrics. At the least of these is corporate and store management skills. But these are manifested in a wide range of factors (e.g., relevance of the store concept, currency of design and environment, intensity of merchandise presentation, competitive prices, and an enjoyable experience, based on great service).

KPI	Typical Ranges	Comments
Sales Related:	**Compare against:**	Measures store increase for stores open over one year. First year or two should be in the +10% to 20% range. Negative; 0 to ±2% is a sign that action needs to be taken. Small increases in the 3% or less range are cause for concern, as inflation runs ±2%. (Note: this can be deflation in some commodities like electronic or apparel)
• Same stores sales increase (e.g., 2% to 5% to 10%) $\text{This year} - \text{last year} = \dfrac{\text{difference}}{\text{Last year}} = \%$ $\$950{,}000 - \$900{,}000 = \dfrac{\$\ 50{,}000}{\$900{,}000} = 5.5\%$	• National and regional data • Total center • Commodity group • Commodity leader • Similar stores or locations	
Sales per square foot: $\dfrac{\text{Store sales year}}{\text{Square footage of store}} = \text{sales per square foot}$ $\dfrac{\$950{,}000}{2{,}500 \text{ sq. ft.}} = \$380 \text{ per square foot}$	• $300 normal • $500 high • $700 exceptional Compare as above	The basic metric for judging store productivity with almost all aspects of store operations and investment affecting it. These will vary by commodity, from high in jewelry (small space with high unit sales); to low in furniture (takes a lot of space) or greeting cards (low unit sales); as well as quality of the center and store location in it.

Source: MOR FOR (Merchandising Operating Results, Financial Operating Results), National Retail Federation.

KPI	Sample Ranges	Comments
Average unit transaction Total sales per year (for day, week) = AUT	Number of transactions per year **Furniture or Jewelry** $\dfrac{\$950,000}{2,000} = \$475.00$ **Greeting Cards** $\dfrac{\$950,000}{200,000} = \$4.75$	Varies widely by commodity from a few transactions, or sales per day for a high-end luxury store, to thousands for a busy drugstore. Increasing average unit sales is an indication of: • Upgrading • Multiple sales per shopper (using multiple unit pricing, e.g., 3 for \$7.99, rather than \$3.00 each) • Effective sales staff • Good product adjacencies • Wide assortments, which encourage a lot of multiple unit sales
Sales per employee Total sales per year Number of full-time equivalent staff	High $980,000 Moderate $500,000 Low $200,000	• Varies widely by commodity and store format (i.e., full service to self-service). Compare to a similar store to determine the effectiveness of total staff.
• Inventory turnover Net sales =T.O. Average year's inventory at retail Year's net sales January to January monthly inventory ÷13	**Typical Range** Low • Jewelry 1–2 • Footwear 2–3 Moderate • Apparel 4–5 • Electronics 6–8 High • Food 12–52	• Industry standard for assessing merchandise flow will vary by commodity. Too high a turnover will likely lead to stock-outs and lost sales, too low will indicate a lot of "dead" inventory and low sales.

Source: MOR FOR (Merchandising Operating Results, Financial Operating Results), National Retail Federation

Balance Sheet and Financial Ratios

The balance sheet provides a financial snapshot of the assets and liabilities of the company and is prepared at least once per year. It is the primary tool, used both internally and externally, to assess the health of a business.

The balance sheet has two sides:

- Assets: listing of assets owned by the company
- Liabilities: outstanding debt owed by the company, and shareholder equity

Retail Balance Sheet (e.g., Successful Supermarket)

Assets		($000)
Current	Cash	$ 686
	Short-term notes	$ 364
	Accounts Receivable	$ 381
	Inventory	$1,310
	Other	$ 175
	Total	$2,916
Long-term	Fixed assets	$4,174
Total		$7,090

Assets

One side of the balance sheet is a list of current and long-term (fixed) assets. Current or short-term assets include cash, accounts receivable, inventory, and anything else that can quickly be turned into cash. Assets are things that the company owns.

The Balance Sheet

Liabilities				($000)
Current	Accounts payable			$2,242
	Income tax due			$ 78
	Bank loan,etc			$ 630
	Debt due in year		$ 259	$3,209
Long-term	Debt (bonds)		$2,684	$5,893
Shareholder Equity	Capital, retained earnings		$3,124	$9,017

Liabilities

The other side of the balance sheet has a list of current and long-term liabilities.

- A liability is something that the company has yet to pay
- Current liabilities are accounts payable (supplier accounts) and outstanding, short-term bank loans
- Long-term liabilities are paid over a longer period (e.g., a ten-year bank loan or mortgage, or leasehold improvements)
- Shareholder equity is the shareholders' investments in the business over the years

A review of a retailer's balance sheet will likely be used only for independents or at the corporate level for chain stores.

Liquidity Ratios

Liquidity ratios reveal the company's short-term ability to meet its financial obligations. They include current and stock-turn ratios. Liquidity ratios include the following:

- Current ratio
- Accounts Receivable ratio
- Profitability and activity ratios
- Gross and net profit margins
- Return on net assets (RONA)

Current Ratio

- The current ratio focuses on the relationship between cash (and "near cash") and short-term obligations
- Current assets include cash, short-term securities, accounts receivable, and inventories
- These last three items are considered "near cash" because they can be quickly converted into cash
- The current ratio relates current assets to current liabilities
  - By the time the value of current assets exceeds the amount of our current liabilities.

    $$\text{Current ratio:} \quad \frac{\text{Current assets} \quad \$2.9M}{\text{Current liabilities} \quad \$3.2M} = .9$$

  - This company has enough cash or "near cash" to meet its short-term financial obligations .9 times. This means that they do not have enough current assets to cover their current liabilities.

Accounts Receivable Ratio

- Number of days' worth of overdue accounts
- The average daily sales (below) is the yearly sales divided by the number of days in the year (365)

A/R days outstanding: $$\frac{\text{Accounts receivable}}{\text{Average daily sales}}$$

A/R days outstanding: $$\frac{\$38M}{(\$57M/365)} = 6.6 \text{ days}$$

- 6.6 days' worth of sales revenue tied up in accounts receivable

Profitability and Activity Ratios

Gross profit margin: $$\frac{\text{Sales} - \text{Cost of Goods Sold}}{\text{Sales}}$$

Gross profit or gross margin %: $$\frac{\$400,000 - \$220,000}{\$400,000} = 45\%$$

Net profit margin: $$\frac{\text{Net profit}}{\text{Sales}}$$

Net profit margin %: $$\frac{\$ 10,000}{\$400,000} = 2.5\%$$

Return on Net Assets (RONA)

- RONA relates net profit to net assets and tells how well the company is using its assets

RONA: $$\frac{\text{Net profit}}{\text{Net assets}} \quad \frac{\$ 473M}{\$3,670M} = 12.9\%$$

- Investment in the company has given a 12.9% return
- A $3,670M investment made $473M.

Global Retailing

In total scope, retailing is a huge industry with the United States dominating both in the number of top 200 retailers (42.5%) and in sales by retailers (50.6%), according to research provided by Deloitte Touche Tohmatsu.

Top 200 Retailers, by Country of Origin

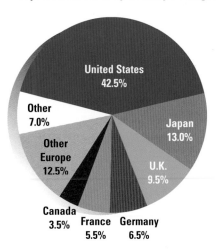

Top 200 Retailers, by Sales

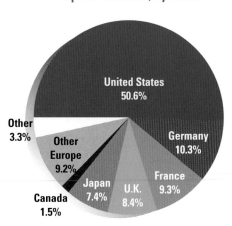

Sector Composition of the Top 200 Retailers

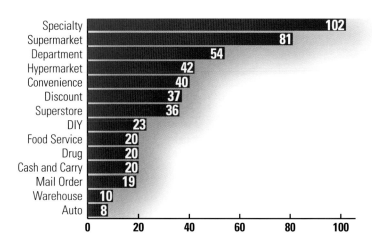

See the Appendix A at the end of this book for a list of the top 200 global retailers.

2. Identifying Weaknesses and Taking Action

Getting to the bottom of why a store is unproductive is a two-phase process. While you may pick up visual hints from observing the stores and shopper traffic, the sales and operating data will give you concrete evidence that something is amiss. Once a problem is confirmed by either the information from the sales reports regarding low or no sales growth compared to other stores in the category, or by KPIs (Key Performance Indicators/Indexes) shared by store management, it is time to drill down to the source of the problem.

When addressing a problem, be sure to do so with professional, objective eyes. It is important to leave your own preferences and biases behind. Your job is to observe the store from the target market segment's viewpoint. This is not always an easy job to do for stores as diverse as children's wear, fast food, or furniture. The following section identifies common trouble spots and offers management, specifically, suggestions for encouraging change and working constructively with their retailers.

What to
Look For

Visual Clues

The Design

- The store has not had a refurbishment, new design, or touch-up for many years.
- Stores that offer the same or similar products are far more appealing.

Worn floors, old fixtures, and poor lighting are a turnoff.

Action

- Address and enforce design standards in the lease.

Note:

At the same time, beware of encouraging over-design. Working on behalf of a large developer, we were asked to review a store in "sales trouble." At a glance it was obvious that this specialty gift shop looked fabulous: deep wool carpet, marble fixtures, costly lighting, and intricate build-out; but there was almost no merchandise. When the owner was broached on the lack of merchandise, she broke into tears. The design called for her to put her investment into bricks and mortar, not merchandise (the heart of retailing). The designer got an award. The tenant went under.

The Messy Store

- A messy store usually reflects the personality of a store and/or regional manager.

It is difficult to find what you want when merchandise is disorganized.

Action

- Discuss the situation, showing the differences between this store and other stores in the center.

- Review with regional management and get agreement on standards.

- Request a change of store management if performance is not up to standard.

Perpetual "On Sale" Signs and Clearances

- Often a sign of weak financial health (cash flow) or poor
  buying and/or selling skills.

A turnoff: all the merchandise that shoppers didn't want at regular price.

Action

- Discuss and get agreement to limit clearances to specific time
  periods.
- Watch for rent payment delay.

Low Depth of Merchandise

- No strong merchandise story.
- Lack of new, hot items; just a mish-mash.

Action

- Take the store manager to visit and discuss fully stocked and
  powerfully merchandised stores versus what this store is doing.
- Determine whether suppliers are being paid promptly.
- Explain that successful stores take a stand with in-depth stock
  on merchandise categories, ideas, and items. Bold statements
  send a message to shoppers that this theme or item is
  important – a "Gee, you should try one of these" message.

There is no way that this store can be productive with this little product at the entrance.

Empty shelves equal low sales per square foot.

Note:

One of our clients bought a gardening store, where each fall they sold bulbs and fertilizer. When analyzing last year's sales, they noticed that the store sold out of fertilizer in several weeks. Because the item was a basic and should sell for as long as the bulbs, they increased their order ten times and created a mass display at the store entrance. The result was a sellout and a big increase in business. There is no risk when the retailer steps in and buys high-demand basics in depth.

Poor Aisle and Traffic Flow Pattern

* Some stores are easy to get into, find what you want, and get out. Others are very convoluted. Research shows that efficiency in shopping has become the determining issue for a lot of consumers, especially the ones who have money to spend and are buying.

Great products, but impossible to get a stroller through this toy store.

Action

- Discuss with store and regional managers to get action. Show them stores that are well organized. Characteristics of a well-designed store include the following:

    — Exterior signs that identify the store at the entrance and at eye level.

    — Windows or entrance displays that send the right message for your target customers.

    — Easy access to entrances.

    — Features of in-depth, high-demand promoted items.

    — Clear aisle patterns.

    — Aisles wide enough for a shopper, plus baby carriages or wheelchairs.

    — Power walls from the entrance featuring high-profit categories.

    — Anchor categories, services, and fitting rooms at the rear of the store with an enticing visual presentation.

    — The service desk in a position that is central to traffic.

- Do an exit interview survey of about 50 shoppers to get their comments and share with the retailer.

Note:

We were asked by a kitchenware store how sales at the rear of their store could be improved. It was suggested that a partition that partially blocked an aisle to the rear be taken down and the aisle to the back be completely opened up. This resulted in a 20% increase in this department.

Merchandise Clues

Stock Outs, Broken Size, or Color Ranges

- Limited selection can suggest a number of things, including an inadequate inventory control system, management passivity, poor planning, lack of proper information technology (IT), and a dysfunctional replenishing system.

Stock-outs frustrate shoppers. They will go elsewhere to find what they need.

Serious problem – empty shelves and stock-outs.

Action

- Determine whether this is an occasional situation or a continuous issue that needs serious attention. If it is continuous, point out that sales are affected and discuss ways of improving planning.

Last or Previous Season's Inventory Is a Retail No-no

- You do not want old inventory hanging around. Disciplined retailers have aged-stock policies and procedures that require in-season markdowns and clearance action on slow sellers.

Is it summer or winter in this store?

Action

- If something is not moving at all, even after price reductions, it should be sent to a clearance or outlet store or given away to a charity shop.
- Point out the competitive disadvantage holding onto old merchandise puts the store in, compared to those with fresh inventory. Show the negative effect by calculating the cost of carrying the dead inventory, compared to moving it out or liquidating it and investing in full-margin product that will sell.

Lack of New Merchandise

- Suggests that management is not on top of merchandise trends, slow in placing orders, overstocked in the wrong products, or having a cash flow/supplier payment problem.

Action

- These can be structural and continuous, or these can be short-term problems. If the former, prepare for trouble ahead. You will need to get answers from buying management.
- If the latter, discuss what caused this problem and learn how the company will move to prevent it from happening again.

Services

Detecting signs of service troubles is not as easy as observing the visual aspects of retailing. Nevertheless, with a keen eye and consistent store visits, the following can be detected:

Poor Quality of Staff

- Staff problems often arise when minimum wage staff are hired without supportive management, training, coaching, and rewards for good performance.

Standards and discipline are needed in the way sales associates dress, conduct themselves, show enthusiasm for their work, and perform basic operational tasks. Stores with poor quality of staff will have low average transactions, few loyal customers, high staff turnover, and low sales productivity.

Action

- Center sales training courses.
- Financial rewards for good performance.

A Lot of Part-time Staff and Too Few Long-service, Full-time Staff

- This is a sign that management is being frugal in the wage budget. Trying to save by hiring too high a portion of part-time staff rarely succeeds and more often leads to a downward spiral in productivity, resulting in store closings.

Action

- Discuss with regional or home office management.
- Review staff scheduling system.

Note:

Using (a lot of) part-time staff in a store does not have to translate into second-rate service. I remember asking a regular part-time woman if she would "manage" a small part of a store. Mrs. Johnson took on this responsibility with great enthusiasm (it elevated her interest and challenged her), with the result that sales took off like a rocket. Both the store and Mrs. Johnson enjoyed an increase.

This type of policy discourages shoppers.

Signs Restricting Returns and Cash Refunds

- Such signs indicate the lack of a consumer-friendly culture, poor cash flow, or an inadequate IT system that monitors and prevents abusive use of returns.

Action

- Center leases should prohibit stores from highly restrictive return and refund policies.
- Discuss the negative implication of one store doing this while its competitors have a shopper-friendly policy.

Lack of "Nice Little Extras"

"Nice Little Extras" include services such as special gift wrapping, product assembly, free beverages for shoppers, shipping anywhere, and ethnic staff where appropriate. By failing to provide any of these, the store is giving the message that it really doesn't care.

Action

- Celebrate those stores in the center that "go the extra mile" and tell anecdotes about how the various low-cost "little extras" help their business (see page 57 for ideas).

Note:

When listening to the leaders of great retail companies, I am always impressed by how their organization encourages bottom-up input and ideas. Part of Starbucks' success is due to the unique products its in-store team members have created – and have been rewarded for, too.

Management

High Turnover of Store Management Can Significantly Hurt a Store's Performance

While change is good and often necessary, whirlwind change can damage the development of a "tried and true" store team. A strong store manager can increase a store's sales by as much as 25%. A weak one can wreak havoc. Effective managers are the type of people you want in your center's stores until they move up the organization ladder. Usually, high turnover of management and staff suggests a dysfunctional culture, likely with the low regard for people and poor pay that go with it. Retailers in this category typically do not last a long time.

This "help wanted" sign is more prominent than the merchandise.

Permanent "Help Wanted/Now Hiring" Signs

- This is a surefire way to tell the world the store has a weak store manager or poor company culture, noncompetitive wages and benefits, or inadequate staff.

Action

- Find out what wages are being paid by other stores and urge the store to pay at least the going rate.

- Spend time to determine if this is a situation caused by store management or if it is chain-wide.

Low Staff Counts at Busy Times:

- Poor staff scheduling system

Action

- Recommend a staff schedule software package.

- If this is a center-wide problem, hold a job fair to help all retailers find good people. Bring in outside specialists to help organize the event and train store managers on hiring best-practices.

Nice-looking store, but no staff.

Financial and Other

Slow or Delayed Rent Payment

- Cash flow problems from low sales, too much inventory, out-of-control expenses, or a chain-wide problem.

Action

- Meet with the appropriate level of management to determine the causes of the problem, and the degree of risk your center faces.
- If chain-wide and your company has a significant downside risk, start action to reduce potential loss.

Slow or Old Technology at Point of Sale

- Management out of sync with new business processes.
- Not using IT effectively.

Action

- Get agreement that there is an issue of concern. Suggest that the store begin an IT review and search that will involve a retail IT consultant.

Store Audit and Retail Satisfaction Programs

Every center should have a two-part retail review program that includes (a) a tenant audit program, and (b) a retail tenant satisfaction survey. By formulating a program of individual store checkups, management will be more likely to spot opportunities and problems in time to take action.

We suggest that the review happen at least quarterly, before each of the major seasonal changes of spring, summer, fall, and winter (Christmas). It should be done individually by the management team, with the audit forms compared, and exceptions discussed and agreed upon. Simply carrying out the review is an excellent development tool because it triggers team discussions and helps educate all the players.

The following forms can be used as checklists for tracking performance. A group of competitive stores in the center can be compared to one another or a single store can be tracked over a period of time.

Store Evaluation by Classification Group

Classification: _____

Date of Evaluation: _____

Evaluation Done By: (Name) _____

Reviewed By: _____

Rate the stores in your mall on a scale of **5 to 1**

5 = Excellent   4 = Good   3 = Average   2 = Fair   1 = Poor

Stores	A	B	C	D	E	Notes
Store						
Sales per sq. ft.						
Convenience of location						
Exterior signage						
Window display						
Façade appeal						
Store Interior						
Cleanliness						
Store layout						
Interior signage						
Lighting						
Overall atmosphere						
Exciting merchandise presentation						
Appeal						
Merchandise suits target market						
Merchandise						
Assortments – breadth						
Assortments – depth						
Range of sizes						
Best sellers featured in depth						
Quality of merchandise						
In-stock position/stock-outs						
Advertised items featured						
Brand names						

Stores	A	B	C	D	E	Notes
Private brands						
No old merchandise						
Merchandise Presentation						
Strong themes identified						
Stock is well organized						
Signs on product features						
Proper lighting						
Price						
Everyday fair prices						
Appropriate price range						
Special sales						
Competitive prices						
Advertising						
Correct creative look						
Involved in center programs						
Good ad support in-store						
Sales and Service						
Number of staff						
Proper approach and skills						
Friendliness of staff						
Appearance / dress						
Knowledgeable of merchandise						
Unlimited guarantee						
Service policies						
Technology						
P.O.S. equipment at service desk						
Wanding at checkout						
Everything bar-coded						
Fast checkout						
Other						
Delivery services						
Exchange/return policy						
Credit/charge accounts						
Clear information in store						

Tenant Audit

This form helps center management analyze a tenant's overall performance and can pinpoint weak spots in the merchant's operation that could develop into more serious problems.

Shopping Center: _____

Evaluator: (Name) _____

Store: _____

10 = Outstanding   1 = Poor

	1st Quarter	2nd Quarter	3rd Quarter	4th Quarter
Store Maintenance				
Storefront: Are all materials in good repair (windows, moldings, flooring, wood trim, etc.) and maintained according to mall standards?				
Interior: Are all materials in good repair (carpeting, fixtures, lighting, counters, etc.) and maintained according to mall standards?				
Overall: Is the store dated-looking in terms of architectural design, décor, and finishing touches?				
Dressing Rooms: Are they sufficient in number, appropriately placed and designed, neat and tidy?				
Stock				
Timelines: Is the stock fresh and current? Does it include important items of the season, trends, and styles?				
Levels: Is the inventory adequate to convince the customer that the shop warrants a visit? Are seasonal inventories adequate?				
Condition/Age: Is there too much "old" merchandise? Is merchandise soiled, damaged, wrinkled, etc.?				
Clearance: Is slow-moving merchandise cleared so current merchandise can be appropriately displayed?				
Merchandise Presentation				
Windows: Does the treatment create interest enough to attract shoppers? Do window displays tell a story? Is each display sensitive to color/design? Is display changed regularly?				

10 = Outstanding   1 = Poor

Merchandise Presentation (Continued)	1st Quarter	2nd Quarter	3rd Quarter	4th Quarter
Entrance: Is it open, uncluttered, and inviting? Do visible displays invite inspection?				
Check Desk: Does the merchandise presentation at the check desk offer additional opportunities for sales? Is it neat and organized?				
Stock Maintenance: Is it straight, orderly, and appealing to the eye?				
In-Store Display: Is it well coordinated, featuring appropriate items, and well lit?				
Display Tools and Their Use: Is there proper signing? Are there sufficient fixtures, mannequins, and lighting?				
Signage: Are advertised items signed, as well as special purchases and promotions? Are the signs properly used?				

Sales Staff

	1st Quarter	2nd Quarter	3rd Quarter	4th Quarter
Appearance: Is personnel appearance in keeping with the store image, i.e., dress, grooming?				
Salesmanship: Do personnel approach, greet, converse, offer selling facts, counter objections, close?				
Friendliness: Are the salespeople warm, interested in the customers and in their needs?				
Knowledge: Are the salespeople trained, knowledgeable about merchandise? Do they use suggestion selling? Do they have a basic knowledge of in-store promotions and advertising?				
Staff Levels: Are there adequate salespeople for the hour, day, season?				

Management

	1st Quarter	2nd Quarter	3rd Quarter	4th Quarter
Attitude: Is the management working toward same profit goals as the mall and the tenant home office? Do they adhere to mall rules? Do they treat customers and staff with respect and consideration? Do they enthusiastically participate in mall programs and promotions?				
Experience: Are they qualified to manage size and type of store? Where are their weak/strong areas? Are they making an effort to learn the job better?				

(Continued)

10 = Outstanding   1 = Poor

Management (Continued)	1st Quarter	2nd Quarter	3rd Quarter	4th Quarter
Turnover: Is there longevity enough to build a trackable management record? If there is high turnover, why? Does the management personality fit with the tenant's retailing philosophy?				
Store Policies: Are they clearly displayed and stated where required?				
Marketing				
Awareness: Is the management aware of the mall marketing program and goals? Do they review promotional flyers, calendars, newsletters, etc.?				
Attitude: Does the tenant view the mall marketing program as an additional sales aid, attempting to tie in with supplemental advertising programs? Are mall programs resented or ineffectively used?				
Participation: Does the tenant take advantage of mall promotions, returning questionnaires, attending mall meetings, making an effort to appropriately stock and display for mall events?				
Lease: Does the tenant make an effort to meet advertising lease agreements? Is the agreement viewed as a marketing aid or a burden?				

Comments, Recommendations, Overall Evaluation of Tenant Operations

Source: ICSC's The Library of Shopping Center Forms.

Retailers' Satisfaction Survey

Feedback provided by this survey will help management determine its strengths and weaknesses. The survey is mailed with an accompanying letter. The letter may be changed for centers other than those acquired in a portfolio.

Today's Date: _____

Tenant Name: _____

Tenant Business Name: _____

Street Address: _____

City: _____ State: _____ ZIP: _____

Dear _____

(Management Co. Name) has been involved with the (Shopping Center Name) for over a year and we are interested in your feedback to determine ways to serve you better. Hopefully, enough time has passed that you have had a chance to get to know the Leasing Representative and the Property Manager for the center and are able to offer us some insights or suggestions for improvement.

Please take a few minutes to complete the enclosed survey and return it in the self-addressed, stamped envelope. The survey may be filled out anonymously, or you may feel free to sign your name at the bottom, whichever is more comfortable for you.

Thank you in advance for your input. I look forward to hearing from you.

Sincerely,

COMPANY NAME
By: Management Company Name: _____

_____

Manager Name: _____

Title: _____

XX:xx

attachment   *(Continued)*

Retailers' Satisfaction Survey

XYZ Management Company
Retailers' Satisfaction Survey

Please circle the letter or check the box that represents the best answer to each question below. If you oversee more than one property, your comments may be given as an overall response.

1. What is your company's type of business? (Check one)
     ☐ clohing   ☐ other retail sales   ☐ food/food service   ☐ other (specify):_____

2. What is your position with the company? (check one)
     ☐ owner   ☐ store manager   ☐ other employee
     ☐ corporate staff (specify):_____   ☐ other (specify):_____

3. How good a job do you think (name of management company) does on the following:

	Poor				Excellent
a. Keeping the parking lot and common areas clean	1	2	3	4	5
b. Ensuring a process to address safety and security concerns	1	2	3	4	5
c. Making repairs to the common areas	1	2	3	4	5
d. Using quality contractors for maintenance	1	2	3	4	5
e. Maintaining a good tenant mix	1	2	3	4	5

4. How many times in the last 12 months have you or someone in your company contacted (name of management company) about a problem (such as billing, maintenance, etc.) with the property you are leasing? (Check one)
     ☐ Fewer than 5 times   ☐ 5 to 10 times   ☐ 10 to 20 times   ☐ More than 20 times

5. Please circle the number that most closely reflects your opinion.

	Strongly Disagree				Strongly Agree
a. (Name of management company) personnel are friendly and treat us politely and with respect	1	2	3	4	5
b. When (name of management company) makes decisions about our property, they explain the decisions clearly	1	2	3	4	5
c. We trust the people we deal with at (name of management company)	1	2	3	4	5
d. (Name of management company) treats us fairly	1	2	3	4	5
e. (Name of management company) listens to us whenever we have a problem or concern	1	2	3	4	5
f. When (name of management company) agrees to solve our problems, it does so quickly	1	2	3	4	5
g. I feel my relationship with (name of management company) is valuable to me	1	2	3	4	5
h. My business is doing as well as projected	1	2	3	4	5

6. How much do you agree with the following statements about your Leasing Representative?

	Strongly Disagree				Strongly Agree
a. Was courteous and friendly	1	2	3	4	5
b. Seemed genuinely happy to have my business	1	2	3	4	5
c. Explained matters so that I could understand	1	2	3	4	5
d. Was responsive to my concerns and questions	1	2	3	4	5
e. Returned my calls promptly	1	2	3	4	5
f. Was interested in understanding my business needs	1	2	3	4	5
g. Worked to reach an agreement that benefited both parties	1	2	3	4	5

7. How much do you agree with the following statements about your Property Manager?

	Strongly Disagree				Strongly Agree
a. Was courteous and friendly	1	2	3	4	5
b. Easy to contact	1	2	3	4	5
c. Returned my calls promptly	1	2	3	4	5
d. Listened to my concerns and problems	1	2	3	4	5
e. Was responsive to my concerns and questions	1	2	3	4	5
f. Followed through on things he/she promises	1	2	3	4	5

8. What do you think (name of management company) does especially well?

_____

_____

9. In what areas do you think (name of management company) needs to improve its performance?

_____

_____

How? _____

_____

_____

Additional comments: _____

_____

_____

(Optional) Name: _____

Thank you in advance for your help on this very important project.

Source: ICSC's The Library of Small Shopping Center Forms.

3. Working with Retailers

The Benefits of Working Together

A commitment to assisting retailers build productivity on an individual basis is not a common policy. Yes, almost all shopping center companies are concerned about their tenants. However, the key question is, just how far should that concern be taken? The answer is a matter of company philosophy and policy.

The philosophies vary. One is: "We've got tens or hundreds of millions of dollars invested in this development, so we must be very sure that the retailers are excellent tenant partners." This approach is embraced by center management to ensure the maintenance of a healthy asset, as well as to keep their tenant partners performing at top levels.

The opposite philosophy is: "We've done our job. We bought the land, paid for the services, built the center, attracted a good mix of tenants, and run our operations well. Our job is done. The retailers seem to know what they're doing, so best stay out of their way." This philosophy espouses a hands-off relationship with little more than standard communications, operations, services, and marketing.

Whatever the approach, keep in mind that the roles of the two parties are played out in a partnership. The retailer reacts to consumer demands on a daily basis and the developer reacts to consumer demands as leases come due – all within the context of the center and its trade area.

The shopping center can perform better if it ensures that its array of retailers are the best there is – in every sense of the phrase. Best means best in the category, best in store environment, best in merchandise, best in service, and best in marketing. Those centers that make the effort to understand retailing, that insist on top performance and support it, will be more productive than those that don't.

Certainly, there will be adversarial issues, but a proactive retailer communication and support program can only help draw in the people who ultimately determine how successful you are – the consumer.

The benefits include:
- knowing a lot about retailing and what retailers do, so centers will be able to react faster to retailer and consumer shopper needs;
- avoiding costly losses of tenants, which hurt both revenues and the center's reputation as a good place to do business;
- keeping local independents and small chains healthy, thereby staying closer to the community and helping to competitively differentiate your property; and
- operating a shopping center that is more vital and competitive than those run in a standard way.

Types of Programs

Think about what kind of tenant support program you want for you shopping center. You might consider anything from an informal approach to a full-fledged resource center staffed by an expert or supported by a consultant and specialists. Either way, keep in mind the following:

1. Purpose

- To help those tenants who are in serious trouble.
- To help those on the borderline from slipping towards failure.
- To help all tenants improve in things from visual presentation to staff selling skills.
- To prevent turnover and vacancies.
- To increase revenue.
- To maintain a mix of local stores.

2. Focus

- Does your plan entail general assistance to all tenants or intense focus on just a few?

3. Level of involvement

Options include:

- Series of educational sessions with attendance not mandatory, (e.g., "Getting Ready for Christmas").
- Focused educational and coaching sessions for pre-selected stores with specific topics (e.g., "Shopper-stopper Windows and Entrance Areas" or "The Seven Steps of Selling").
- A coaching and improvement action program with structured follow-up for individual retailers.

4. Retailer review

- No matter what level of commitment, the center should have a program that keeps an objective eye on all tenants. This goes beyond the daily walkthrough to include a high-quality tracking audit linked to sales reports. (See pages 34-41.) Needless to say, if stores report significant decreases, an immediate review should be conducted.

The tracking audit and sales report analysis can pinpoint trouble early so that the center management can get on the problem immediately. When chains are involved, the report can go straight to the head office retail liaison person.

Knowing Who to Assist

Center management can be faced with a dilemma: which retailer(s) to work with. It often happens that the retailers needing immediate help are the least receptive, while those keen for center support are doing well. In these situations, it is critical to both players' success that the people needing your center's help are enthusiastic about the opportunity.

One option for the Tenant Support Program is to run all program levels, namely:

- General educational sessions.
- Focused educational sessions.
- Specific tenant coaching and action programs.

Experience has shown that attendance at educational workshops is higher when:

- they are held one hour before center opening;
- beverages and snacks are served;
- the program is part of a series (e.g., "Our Center College");
- a certificate or reward is given to regular participants;
- the regional or home office management is advised, invited, and asked to get store managers and their team to attend;
- expert speakers give presentations; and
- some fun and networking are added.

Word-of-mouth spreads quickly that these events are very worthwhile to attend.

Selecting which stores to involve in a coaching program depends on several factors:

a) How important the store is to the center's success and need for diversity weighed against how badly the store is doing.

b) The tenant has "gotta wanna": It has to make an all-out effort to change, improve, and commit resources to becoming truly excellent. This commitment must show in the owner's willingness to acknowledge weaknesses, recognize that competitors are doing a better job, and pledge to make sacrifices of time and energy to figure out how to rejuvenate the business.

c) Setting mutually agreed-on action points and goals with a follow-up system to monitor progress, and a "Plan B" if targets are missed.

d) Identifying the amount of resources to get the tasks done (e.g., reduce and sell $25,000 of old inventory to free up cash for buying bestselling items by a certain date).

e) If outside consultants are used, the tenant agrees to pay some percentage (even if only 25%) of the fees as a sign of their commitment. The psychology behind this is that clearly one listens better when one is paying for the advice.

Note:

In working on our Store Doctor® Program, we encountered a wide range of responses to retailer coaching programs. The two most important determinants of success appear to be (a) the tenants' willingness to try to change, and (b) a disciplined follow-up system that monitors the tenants' activity against agreed-upon action steps.

**Role of Center
Management**

Think of the shopping center managers as the quarterbacks for a tenant support program. But they are quarterbacks with a huge support network. They have at their disposal assistant managers, operations and services managers, marketing, security staff, plus the resources of outside experts in retail consulting. They can also call upon sales and service, information technology, help in visual presentation, store design and fixturing, human resources, and merchandising. Again, only if all the available resources are used; no matter how good that quarterback is on his or her own, without the help of the team, there will be no touchdowns.

**Motivating
Change**

The enthusiasm range of store managers in your shopping center will vary. Don't expect everyone to embrace suggestions for improvements to the same degree. Even stores that are suffering serious financial problems often resist suggestions or intervention, and are paralyzed with anxiety over their business situation.

Discussing the need for change and then actually motivating it can involve several approaches:

- **Incentives:** Offer incentives such as rent relief, awards, recognition, or assistance with marketing for resolving negative issues.
- **Special Help:** from the resource centers to assist store management with a specific problem like finding better staff or improving visual presentation.
- **Extra Personal Attention:** from center management to give support when regional management or business supporters of an independent store are not readily available.

Talking Retail

Effective communication means knowing how to talk the language of those with whom you're communicating. Learn the language of retail tenants. Get familiar with retail terms, key performance indicators and measurements, operating and financial ratios, and business words and phrases. You can consult the Resources section of this book. As well, attend at least one retail conference per year to stay on top of trends and identify up-and-coming stores. Most importantly, spend time with your tenants and *listen*. What you will find over time is that listening builds trust. Only then will your ideas and suggestions be accepted by your tenants. Work to gain the endorsement from one tenant and build on that. Soon you'll be able to go to another and say, "Ask the manager of XYZ store, she'll tell you how this idea worked for her." Confidence building, trust building, team building.

Checklist for Establishing Effective Communications

This checklist provides guidelines for communicating effectively.

- Adopt a philosophy that embraces open, honest dialogue.
- Ensure that managers, leasing agents, and all corporate associates who interact with retailers-tenants receive training in positive communication skills.
- When time or distance allows, prioritize tenant communication as follows:
  — Communicate in person
  — Communicate over the phone
  — Communicate via friendly fax (handwritten note preferred)
  — Communicate by typed fax
  — Communicate by handwritten note via mail
  — Communicate by typed formal letter via mail
  — Communicate via registered mail, using legal terms in abundance

- Provide as much information as you can concerning expectations. This will minimize the number of "problem" communications.

- Look for common ground; being right never solved a problem.

- Always accept responsibility for "closing the loop" in communications with tenants and others. Be sure to get back to them and do what was to be done.

- Seek to understand why the communication is taking place. Is it problem-related? If so, look for a systemic solution, one that can be applied to all similar problems, rather than a specific, temporary fix.

Using Outside Experts

Many shopping centers use outside experts. This is done for the following reasons:

- The center management company doesn't have the in-depth, practical "been there and done that" knowledge and experience.

- It is more cost-effective to use outsiders than to maintain this type of expertise on the payroll.

- Outsiders don't come with preconceptions, and tenants are often more willing to listen to suggestions from them.

- Consultants offer advice and expertise to both tenants and the center, so the change is more equitable and not perceived as one-way or punative.

In assessing the use of retail consultants with niche expertise in areas like sales, training and visual presentation, look for the following:

- Do they have years under their belts as managers or employees of a store? If they haven't, it will show up quickly and

credibility will be lost.

- Are they good listeners and communicators?
- Are their reports professional, prescriptive, and practical?
- Do they have good references?
- Do they stick to the schedule, do proper follow-up, and genuinely show an interest in your tenants?

Depending on whether this expertise is for a group or an individual store, the fees can be costly; however, it is an investment in both your center (for better revenues) and the long-term goodwill with your tenants.

Even a retailer in serious financial trouble should consider paying, or committing to pay in the future if she or he is unable to do now, a portion of the expense of one-to-one coaching. Agreeing to pay shows seriousness of intent.

4. Improving Productivity with Training and Service Programs

What Do Shoppers Want?

The key to great service is the right attitude. For shopping center management that means mixing and mingling with your tenants, being accessible. This is called "management by walking around" or MBWA. All great generals throughout history lived with their troops and rallied them. You cannot expect your retail tenants to perform at top levels without your encouragement.

Use the following checklist to test your attitude:

A Customer Respect Checklist for Your Shopping Center [*]

1. **Do we trust our customers?** Do we operate our business to effectively serve the vast majority of customers who are honest, or to protect ourselves from the small minority who are not?

2. **Do we stand behind what we sell?** Are we easy to do business with if a customer experiences a problem with our tenants' offerings? Are front-line employees empowered to respond appropriately to a problem? Do we guarantee the goods we sell? Do we believe in our service?

3. **Do we stress promise-keeping in our company?** Is keeping commitments to customers – from having stores open and close on time to having exceptional washrooms – deemed important to our company?

4. **Do we value our customers' time?** Do we anticipate peak demand periods and staff so as to minimize customer waiting? Are our facilities, parking, and service systems convenient and efficient for customers to use? Do we help prepare new employees to provide efficient, effective service before putting

[*] Leonard L. Berry, Center for Retailing Studies, Texas A & M University

them in front of customers? Do we teach employees that serving customers supersedes all other priorities, such as paperwork?

5.   **Do we communicate with customers respectfully?** Are our signs informative and helpful? Are our statements clear and understandable? Is our advertising above reproach in its truthfulness and taste? Are our contact personnel professional in appearance and manner? Does our language convey respect, such as "I will be happy to do this" and "It will be my pleasure"? Do we answer and return telephone calls promptly, and with a smile in our voice? Is our voice mail system caller-friendly? Is our website easy to navigate?

6.   **Do we respect all customers?** Do we treat all customers with respect, regardless of their appearance, age, race, status, or size of purchase or account? Have we taken any special precautions to minimize discriminatory treatment of certain customers? Are we considerate of seniors and people with disabilities? Are the signing and service desks multilingual?

7.   **Do we thank customers for their business?** Do we say "thank you" at a time other than after a purchase? Do we help our customers feel appreciated?

8.   **Do we respect our employees?** Do our human resources policies and practices pass the employee-respect test? Do our employees, who are expected to respect customers, experience respectful treatment themselves? Would employees want their children to work in our company when they grow up?

Here is another excellent list of service standards:

Ten Determinants of Quality Service

How to improve service is the #1 priority for most shopping centers and retailers. Here is a rundown on what determines good-quality service. Use these 10 points as the basis for weekly staff meetings, and as part of your "talk the talk, walk the walk." Retailers should talk to their team of sales associates about what each topic means to them and share anecdotes on personal experiences. Have them suggest policies and practices to put in place for their store.

1. **Reliability** – consistency in performing the service right from the start.
2. **Responsiveness** – willingness and readiness of employees to provide service.
3. **Competence** – possessing the skills and knowledge required to perform the service.
4. **Access** – approachability/ease of contact between associates and customers.
5. **Courtesy** – politeness, respect, consideration, and friendliness of personnel contact.
6. **Communication** –listening to tenants and customers; talking in a language they can relate to.
7. **Credibility** – trustworthiness, believability, honesty, and having the tenants' and shoppers' best interest at heart.
8. **Security** – freedom from danger, risk, or doubt.
9. **Empathy for the customer** – making the effort to understand the tenants' and customer's needs.
10. **Tangibles** – hard evidence of service: physical facilities, appearance of personnel, tools or equipment used to provide service, and "look" of the service.

"Customers perceive service quality as the meshing of the service they anticipate and the service they get. It's the balancing of expectations against performance."

– Valarie Z. Zeithmal, Duke University

Center management should set an example and abide by the same creativity and commitment they expect of their retailers.

Breadth and
Range of Services

The suitable range and depth of services will depend on your shopping center's:

- **target market segment(s),** whether it be upper income, young families, urban ethnic groups, etc.;
- **type and mix of stores,** like high-end designers, or a power or lifestyle center, and the number of tenants and so on; and
- **strategic market positioning,** namely super-full-service, discount and restricted services, specialty services, etc.

When leasing, tenants need to clearly understand the center's strategic market position, the role of service(s), and what is required of the tenants in the lease. It's a cliché, but never has it been truer: the chain is only as strong as its weakest link.

Efficient and welcoming
service center.

A Source of Special Service Ideas

The following is a checklist for both the shopping center and individual retailers:

	Your Center	Your Retailers
• A concierge service that delivers anything your customers want		
• Coat and package checking		
• Gift wrap – basic is free, fancy is $5 to charity		
• Delivery and mailing to anywhere		
• Strollers and wheelchairs		
• Tourist information, travel information		
• Multilingual staff		
• Shuttle service to local hotel or transit center		
• Reservation and restaurant guide		
• Child care – from a crèche to a box in the corner full of toys to play with while Mom shops		
• Coffee, tea, herbal teas, juices – free, of course		
• Wine bar		
• Infant change table and diapers		
• Deluxe restroom		
• Vibrating chairs, foot vibrators for tired shoppers		
• "No hassle" guarantee, including "we're sorry" rebate for transit or gas expense for returning problem merchandise		
• Personal shopper, fashion/wardrobe/home design/home workshop counseling		
• Technical information expert for home do-it-yourself projects		
• Special washrooms, telephones, drinking fountains		
• Chairs, benches		
• Product information center		
• Simple signage and guides – large, easy-to-read type		
• Restaurant, café, snack bar, refreshment stand		
• Problem-solving center		
• Parking, easy access to exit		
• Valet car parking		
• Computer/Blackberry access in mall (Wi-Fi)		
• Parcel carrying to car		
• Snow removal and battery recharges for parked cars in winter weather		
• Soft and up-beat music		
• How-to seminars: Build a Deck, Start a Book Collection, Coordinate Your Wardrobe		
• Simple customer satisfaction questionnaire in every parcel		
• Post office, ATM, government service center		
• "How-to" library, classes, and workshops with free take-home videos		
• Special orders		
• Computerized bridal registry		
• Computerized touch screen gift suggestions		
• Computerized store directory with a "destination" map		
• Layaway, Christmas Club		
Your ideas:		
•		
•		
•		
•		

Strong emphasis on custom orders.

Both the customer and the sales associates can see the gift registry. Good use of technology.

A storytelling corner in a bookstore.

Refreshment bar in this upmarket men's store is an appropriate detail.

A play area sends a "we care about you" message, and also facilitates sales service.

Chairs allow shopping partners a chance to rest and gives sales associates a chance to close the sale.

Quality of Service   The challenge of offering great service is when it's consistent, it becomes the norm. If it's better than the competition, people expect it from you. Upping the ante, therefore, may seem like an impossibility: how do you turn great into greater? But remember, the commitment must go beyond simply being great; your stores must commit to a) being leaders in service and b) a formal program of listening to and observing the target shopper. Consumers' needs change, and only by responding accurately, creatively and faster than the competition will a store become and remain a leader. Probing for service issues and needs should be part of your center's market research programs, as well as when you are walking the center.

Raising the Bar

Shopping center management and retailers should be encouraged to conduct a competitive audit of all shopping centers in your trading area, as well as ones that are well known for being industry leaders. Then draw up your:

- service strategy,
- priority activities,
- communication plans,
- implementation plan,
- research program to monitor shopper feedback, and
- plans to continually upgrade the program.

Involving tenants should be continuous. The technique your shopping center uses can include:

- continued reminders through newsletters and store visits of the center's programs and standards;
- regular highlighting of superior store performance and appreciation letters from customers at monthly or annual

meetings, with rewards;

- a program of mystery shoppers that track and report performance (contract with a market research firm to provide a program of secret shoppers, say one per store per month, and more for poor-performing tenants, to track the quality of retailer sales service in your center);
- informing home and regional offices of the programs and their store's performance; and,
- one-on-one meetings with regional or home office involvement to address ongoing complaints.

If your center has regular manager and staff training meetings, make sure to include time for a brief report and anecdotes from store staff where service is exceptional.

Training Programs   Many centers debate the idea of a regular program for training store management and key staff. The arguments against a regular program often include:

- "The chains have their own program."

True, but many don't.

- "We don't have many independents."

So do it for the ones that you do have, and the best chain store managers will attend, too.

- "Attendance is weak."

A clear sign that your program needs life added to it.

On the other hand, the case for a regular service and retail knowledge program is compelling:

- It's the right thing to do if you really care about your retailers and shoppers.

- Management and staff turnover in retailing is unfortunately often high, so a continuous program of skill development is needed.
- There are always new ideas to be shared, and many firms do not have a mechanism to encourage this.

Here are some suggested guidelines:

- Plan a program for a year, with three or four training sessions in the spring and three or four leading up to Christmas;
- Have a program of topics that builds one upon another towards a learning goal;
- Give it a name (e.g., Retail College), give out a manual, plus a certificate of attendance and recognition;
- Use dynamic, first-class speakers – they motivate and attract more attendees;
- Inform regional or home offices and ask for their support and attendance;
- Keep track of who attends, so you can ask people when they request rent relief, "Why weren't you there?" That will motivate them to come next time;
- Create an enticing invitation and a reminder one to two days before the event;
- Hold the meetings one hour before store opening, keep them to 45 minutes and have good food and beverages available;
- Allow 10 to 15 minutes for audience participation, plus a Q-and-A session; and,
- Send out a follow-up newsletter outlining what the speaker said; this provides both a refresher for those who attended and a reminder for those who didn't.

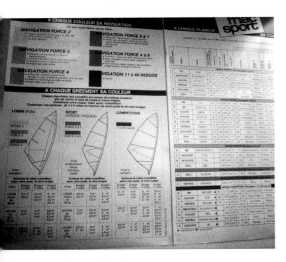

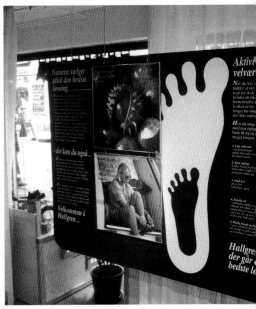

Great product signage supports training and the sales process.

Measuring the Impact of Great Service

Retailing essentially boils down to increasing your share of market day-to-day, hour-by-hour, one-customer-at-a-time.

Simply put, everyone's goal is to create, hold, nurture, and keep customers for life.

Studies show that the cost of contacting, attracting, and selling *new* customers is very unprofitable. However, satisfied customers who return regularly become very profitable. Do all you can to hang on to them. The more effort stores expend on maintaining and building sales with current customers, the more successful they will be. Increasing the number of loyal customers should be a goal.

Value of a Lifetime Customer

The worth of a customer for life to a store is suggested below:

	Average Annual Expenditure	X	Number of Years Per Customer	=	Total Sales Value of a Customer for Life
Bookstore	$ 500	X	10 years	=	$ 5,000
Hardware store	$ 600	X	8 years	=	$ 4,800
Shoes	$ 300	X	8 years	=	$ 2,400
Groceries	$5,200	X	10 years	=	$52,000
Department store	$2,000	X	40 years	=	$80,000
Apparel	$1,000	X	12 years	=	$12,000

How should shoppers be treated when they walk through your door? Like a one-time $20 transaction, or a potential $250,000 customer for life with an asset value of approximately the same amount? Think about it.

Also keep in mind that each customer you consistently treat with superior service will become an "apostle" and tell other people. Your service policy will become your competitive advantage.

Note:

We checked up on one retailer that was tracking well ahead of the rest of the stores in its category group. Their success boiled down to a few simple service programs:

1. They always have a greeter at the door at busy times and a staff member near the door at slower times.

2. The greeter offers the shopper an elegant shopping basket, which increased average unit sales by 20%.

3. They had a fantastic gift wrap service. People shopped there just for this, and the fee was donated to a community charity.

Simple, unique, and effective!

5. Improving Sales with Better Merchandising

Merchandise is the heart of retailing. A store can be in the right location, have a great design, be staffed well and marketed aggressively; but without a healthy core of the right merchandise, all of these other features can only help so much.

Store Focus and Merchandise Strengths

To improve tenants' productivity with better merchandising techniques, stores must develop a strategic focus. This should be based on the following principles:

- A very clear definition of the target market segment that includes demographics and psychographics (lifestyle, attitudes, and shopping behavior information).
- One or two of the Four Es Solutions (page 3). Ensure that the merchandise assortments emphasize either economy or price saving; efficiency with either highly edited or very broad assortments (which translates into a convenience type of assortment or into classification dominance – "we've got it all, so this is the only place to go"); ego and status-enhancing brands; or entertaining and educational products.
- Ranges of products that are as unique as possible so that there is a compelling reason to shop the store.

A broad assortment of unique products is a powerful shopper draw.

In assessing stores in your center, you will find that many do not have:

- a clear focus that translates into a special visual point of view;
- unique products that make the store a destination; and,
- only in-season merchandise, with no dead-end inventory.

Despite the number of stores described above, shopping center management must be very wary of suggesting that a retailer buy specific types of merchandise. This is *not* center management's expertise, even if the idea may seem obvious. Furthermore, if management gives advice and the store takes it and the idea fails, it's the center that "owns" the mistake. Uncomfortable, yet legitimate questions arise, like, should the retailer be compensated for the lost investment?

Inventory Management

An area into which shopping center management should inquire when helping retailers improve productivity is the company's inventory management systems. Chains will likely have their own sophisticated systems with up-to-date point-of-sale equipment and software programs that are organized at the home office.

However, some small chains and independents may not have adequate business processes. There is a huge range of options, which complicates the choice. However, the cost of installing and upgrading IT equipment and software is reasonable. It can often be leased with low monthly payments.

High in-stock levels increase sales and customer satisfaction.

In assessing merchandise productivity, here are some issues to address:

- Is there a timely and continuous flow of new merchandise into the store?
  - Good retailers avoid excessive peaks and valleys of inventory.
- Is the store or company always in an open-to-buy position?
  - If so, they can buy what is needed. If not, there are no funds for hot new items or repeat orders of bestsellers and sales will drop.
- What is selling?
  - If the answer is "a bit of everything," then the retailer may be in trouble and may not be on top of their inventory and operations.
- What are the hot items?
  - A retailing rule is that 80% of sales come from 20% of inventory. These bestsellers (20% of items) must be identified, in stock, and featured. If not, weak sales will follow.

- Are slow sellers quickly identified, marked down in price, and moved out?
  — By clearing out slow-moving inventory, the retailer has funds to buy more of what is selling. The best way to deal with a "home office" that is reluctant is to take the manager to a competitive store and show him or her that their store is not reacting to competitors. Then take digital pictures of this situation and send it to regional and home office executives.
- What is your in-stock position (percentage of items) for the basic, must-have inventory?
  — Efficient operators target 95% (5% of items are sold out and not in stock) and know that this is key to store productivity. If a store doesn't have a wanted item, the customer can't buy it and will go to another shop or center – perhaps for good. Lose a sale and you risk losing a customer.

Guidelines for Power Merchandising for a More Productive Store

No matter which strategy a store chooses, it should offer shoppers an intense merchandising experience because:

- a well-stocked store sends a message of success, which reassures customers;
- stores need high sales, which can only come from a lot of product, to cover high expenses and occupancy costs; and,
- the more merchandise in stock, the more efficient your customers' shopping trips will be.

By following these guidelines, a store can become more vital and focused. Its personality will be crystal clear to its target market and send out a "we're right for you" message.

Follow the Three 'I's – Identify, Isolate, and Intensify.

1. **Identify the store's merchandise position on a daily basis** with systems which record sales and inventory by merchandise departments and classifications. Manage them to the finest possible level of detail, for example, by the stock keeping unit or SKU.

2. **Isolate** those categories and subcategories with sales above or below the store average. Take action by reducing the inventory investment (depth of stock or breadth of assortment) on slow-selling classifications and clear out slow sellers.

3. **Intensify** the breadth and depth of fast-selling categories and items, and invest more in the high-demand departments. Focus on:

- increasing inventory depth on bestsellers
- "exploding" assortment classifications and subclassifications by offering more similar products; and,
- eliminating fringe items – those that collectively account for less than 10% of classification sales. Reinvest the freed-up funds in high-demand classifications.

Stores that have completed this analysis and taken action have strengthened their specialty position and have seen sales and profits increase dramatically.

Note:

A designer boutique carried a few of everything the designer made such as dresses, coats, all casual sportswear, and even ball gowns, sunglasses, swimwear and jewelry. Sales were stagnant, markup was 55%, but markdowns were so high that the gross margin was 36% and inventory turnover was just 3.4.

They were encouraged to take a risk. All fringe categories were dropped and 50% of the inventory went to color-coordinated sweaters, plus skirts, pants, and casual dresses. The store went from being a generalist to a specialist. Sales rose 20% over two years. Gross margin went to 44% and turnover went to 6.0.

**Getting
Department and
Classification
Emphasis Right**

Another reason a retailer's performance can be below par is a lack of understanding of what is driving sales and failure to allocate space in relation to potential. Retailers should regularly conduct reviews of their space. Turn to sales data to help in the assessments and figure out how to reorganize floor, shelf and wall space to maximize allocation of hot-selling items.

**How to Make
Stores More
Productive**

Smart retailers will determine the size and configuration of the store by department, category, and item by item (i.e., how much floor, fixture, and wall space each SKU requires); assign minimum space for the stockroom or non-sales-productive areas; and use this information in a careful analysis of what is and is not selling. There are several software programs available that help in merchandise space planning by translating unit sales into the appropriate sales space for each category and item.

Key Classification Issues to Address

By taking the following approach to store planning, sales and gross margin can be increased up to 20%. The basic principle is "go with the flow." Keep the store flexible and fluid so that the presentation of products is always adjusting to customers' demands.

The following form can be used to help stores think and plan to emphasize successes and get away from low-demand products:

1. Strong classifications that should be expanded

Classification/Category	Current Size	Approximate Future Size
_____	_____ sq. ft.	_____ sq. ft.
_____	_____	_____
_____	_____	_____

Will it be on the power walls or aisles? _____   Where? _____

2. Classifications that can be dropped

Dropped

_____	_____ sq. ft.	_____ sq. ft.
_____	_____	_____

Reduced

_____	_____ sq. ft.	_____ sq. ft.
_____	_____	_____

3. Classifications larger and better than competitors

Competitor	Size of Classification	Number of SKUs
_____	_____ sq. ft.	_____

Our Store:

_____	_____	_____
_____	_____	_____

4. Classifications of Major Product Groups:

Destination Products	**Seasonal**	**Power Wall(s) Aisle(s)**
shoppers will find (e.g., shoes, pet shop, children's or reference books)	new arrivals, seasonal gifts	
_____	_____	_____
_____	_____	_____
_____	_____	_____

The answer to #4 should guide the store layout:

- Destination is used as a magnet or draw.

- Power walls will feature the strength and sell "tonnage."

- Impulse buys should be best sellers or pickup items located at end aisles or the service desk.

- Seasonal items should always be front and forward to catch shoppers' eyes. There should be a program to change this area every two weeks, or more often at Christmas.

Above:
Well-organized, broad, in-depth assortment.

Above, right:
Bestsellers at the entrance and as you exit.

Note:

One store had a change of management. The new manager was still getting organized, and made the mistake of placing two large repeat orders for a best-selling item. He discovered this after it was too late to cancel the order. So this double quantity was featured at the store front, with signs and support staff. The item looked important, sold well, and had to be repeated again. Store sales were great.

6. Improving Productivity with Visual Presentation

Within every center, each retail tenant is in a competitive battle to capture the eye of passing shoppers, lure them into the store, and entice them to buy. The more stores doing a good job of this, the better it is for both the landlord and the retailer. Great shopping environments thrive on strong competitors clustered together to offer an enticing shopping experience.

An intensely proactive store design review should be conducted as part of the leasing and renewal activity. It is paramount to both the shopping center and the retailer that the visual impact of each store be:

- effective at attracting shoppers;
- reflective of the quality of the center and what the store brand stands for;
- unique, so that the total center experience is special and interesting; and,
- up-to-date with both in-center and non-center trends and competition.

Management should keep on top of weak-impact retailers who can detract from the total center's environment and experience and pull other retailers down.

Powerful Exterior Impact

At best, retailers have about three to five seconds to catch shoppers' eyes as they approach and view the windows and entrance. Try standing outside both a high- and low-productivity store and watch the passing shoppers' body movements. Note the percentage that don't take notice, or just glance and move on. This is a very simple way of witnessing why effective signage, exterior design, windows, and presentation at entrances are so important to a store's productivity. If you cannot lure them in, they are not going to buy.

Here are the areas to address:

Store Front

Does your store front tell customers what the store is all about and reach out to the store's target market? Does it project a unique personality?

Above:
Fun and animation draw
shoppers' attention.

Above, right:
Now they are open for
business!

Right:
It is easy to understand
what this store sells.

Store Signs

- Does it stand out in the crowd of competitors' signs?
- Does it reflect the style used in advertising and other communications?
- Does it work day and night, summer and winter?
- Is it appealing to the target market?
- Is the store name at eye level in the window?
- Is the store front well maintained?

This design is all part of building a strong brand image.

No one is going to miss this sign.

Windows

Is there a simple, yet captivating merchandising message that a passing shopper can understand within a second or two?

- Is the merchandising message compelling, carrying a "take another look" appeal?
- Are the merchandise signs in the windows easy to read?
- Is the merchandise priced on the signs or smaller tickets so that people who do stop can determine if the price is right for them?
- Are the windows and doors clutter-free?

Above:
Eye-level appeal, plus good signs.

Above, right:
Very creative use of cutlery to demonstrate the store's product strength.

Right:
A simple message you "get" in a second or two.

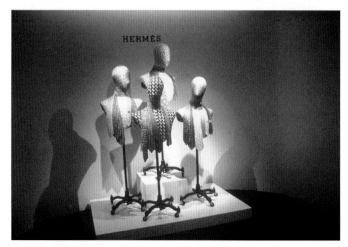

Entrance

- Is the entrance barrier free?
- Is there a merchandise theme in a "front and forward" position that builds upon the merchandise theme in the windows?
- Is the front-and-forward merchandise feature just behind the "decompressor zone"? (This is at the immediate entrance to allow shoppers a brief moment to slow down and adjust to being inside the store.)
- Is it easy to visually sweep the store with one's eye in order to understand what the store is all about?
- Does someone greet people at the entrance?
- Is the entrance free of intimidating signs like "No shirt, no shoes, no service," or "Shoplifters will be prosecuted"?
- Is there a place for a community notice board or a sign communicating the store's neighborhood involvement?
- Can the other senses be aroused? (e.g., pleasant aroma from café or perfumery; interesting music from an electronics store; exciting nonstop video or plasma screen in a sporting goods store, or of a fashion show in a designer boutique.)
- Is there appropriate floor covering to convey an important message about your store's identity? For example, deep carpeting for luxury or basic concrete for cost savings.
- Are you playing music to create the right mood?

Below, left:
Leading off with color and merchandise impact.

Below, right:
No doubt about what this store's key item is — one sweater in 16 colors, "WOW!"

Productive

Layouts

Once the shopper is inside the store, the combination of store layout and visual attraction takes over. A productive store is a store where shoppers can find what they are looking for *efficiently*. More and more, research indicates that time, convenience, and efficiency are of growing importance to the majority of consumers, especially to the ones with high disposable income. If customers find shopping in a store a pleasant, time-saving experience, they will return time and again.

Making a Store Layout More Efficient

No matter what a retailer's prime business or service strategy is, an enjoyable and efficient experience starts with the store's layout. The key components of an efficient layout are:

- ease of getting in, around, and out;
- simple aisle patterns and comfortable widths;
- logical location of merchandise, service areas, and support areas; and,
- flexibility for seasonal merchandise and consumer changes.

Clear aisle patterns encourage shoppers to enter.

You just know that they do well.

Store Layout Diagram

Four major layout grids merit consideration, namely:

- the Rectangle/Loop
- the Gridiron
- the Open Flow, and
- the Main Aisle.

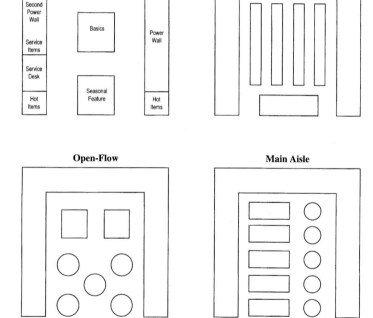

All four layout options follow the same basic principles:

- Position seasonal, high gross margin and high-demand items at the front at eye level.
- Display related products together to show merchandise strengths. This encourages multiple item sales.
- Keep stockroom and office space to a minimum, about 10% of the store's total space at most.

- Choose a layout and visual strategy that support and communicate the retailer's key strategy.
- Within the layout plan, allow merchandising and promotion flexibility.

Tips on Store Design

A great new store upgrade can increase sales by 20 to 30%. When guiding retailers on store design, suggest that they:

- visit stores they like, ask about the designer and if s/he worked out well, and interview that designer and two others.
- be sure to talk about sales productivity per square foot and not just about a wonderful design.
- state clearly what the core strategy is, how design should support it, what goes where and why, and what the specific budget is.
- show their initial sketches and designs to staff and customers for feedback.
- Judge their work based on:
    - supporting your strategic direction;
    - appealing to your target market;
    - creating a unique image different from the competition;
    - showing merchandise and supporting service;
    - a design that can come in on budget; and,
    - the likelihood of achieving high sales per square foot.

Note:

Not all new store designs work! Recently, a national brand apparel chain decided to update their look from a "heart of America" appeal to being very "hip and cool." The results were disastrous – a 20% sales decrease. Fortunately, this was done in a test store, and they went back to the drawing board.

Helping Stores Become Highly Productive

How does a store become highly productive or profitable? Here are a few tips on the physical side of this question.

- Measure sales per square foot by:
  - store total.
  - department, classification or category (to identify high and low producers).
  - area of the store – front, side walls, "power walls," central area, and back end. The first 25% of a specialty store should generate close to 50% of sales. The back end should act as an anchor or the place to find basic products.
  - seasonal changes.
- Measure sales per linear shelf foot to determine how productive the fixtures are. There will not be industry data or standards on this, so establish benchmarks for sales per linear foot of shelf space based on (a) location in store or department, (b) level of shelf (e.g., eye level, mid-fixture, or up high or very low). Note: "Sales per linear shelf foot" is measured in terms of the frontage of fixture shelving. If you have one fixture or wall with four shelves, each eight feet long, then there will be 32 linear shelf feet. The shelf feet at eye level should produce many times more sales (per shelf foot) than those above or below eye level.
- Can walls and fixtures be heightened to increase the intensity of merchandise inventory per square foot?
- Do the windows, store façade, signs, and entrance entice and capture passing traffic by clearly sending a "look at me" message that tells shoppers what the store is and that there is interesting merchandise inside?

The Key to Productivity Is Flexibility

Winning stores will have a store layout, fixturing, and presentation system that is flexible. We all know how customers' demands change; stores must be able to adjust and change with them. But to do this, you need information on how to react and manage change. Remember the three I's – Identify, Isolate, and Intensify (page 69). All three must be done to merchandise assortments by store, classification, category, and SKU.

As classifications and items grow or fade in importance, the space allocated to them should reflect this. Here's how:

1. Start by shrinking weak classifications.
2. Mark down and drop slow sellers.
3. Expand the depth and number of shelf facings for bestsellers.
4. Set up hot spots at high traffic areas, windows, and entrances for exceptional items.
5. Use height in relation to presenting merchandise at eye level. The more merchandise you can position at a relatively high level, the greater your profitable sales volume will be. Feature high-selling, high gross margin merchandise at eye level.

Complete a Plan-O-Gram to Increase Productivity Through Planning

Store management should sit down and work out a plan on how the store will present itself to the customer on a department, classification, category, and item basis. By careful planning, allocation, measurement, and evaluation of selling space usage, retailers can make dramatic improvements in sales, inventory turnover, and profit.

Example of a simple plan-o-gram

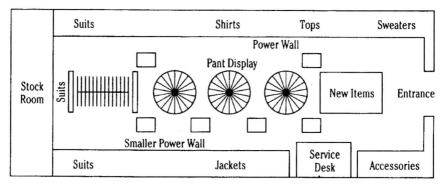

Men's Shop Floor Plan: Complete one for each season.

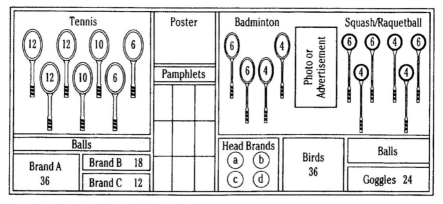

Sporting Goods Store: Racquet Section.
Complete in detail for each sport season. List the exact item and quantity for each space.

Fixtures

While fixturing is an area that offers an almost unlimited range of choice, there are some basic features that all good fixturing includes, namely:

- the ability to hold ample merchandise,
- be signed and ticketed so that identifying the wanted item is easy,
- be easy to maintain, and
- be easy to move (where required).

Fixtures have not changed radically over the past half-century. There are examples of more merchandise being shown on higher walls used as backup stock, but there are also many stores with fixtures virtually the same as in historic pictures of John Wanamaker's or Marshall Field's department stores.

What is important is that the store has a clear rational for using the types of fixtures it has. This doesn't mean copying competitors; even within the same industry sectors there are different approaches. Wal-Mart, for instance, has high fixtures and aisles filled with pallets of "specials"; Target, on the other hand, has lower fixtures and clean aisles. Both do very well. Good fixturing must allow flexibility.

Why not use the floors, tables, fixtures, and walls?

Fixtures on wheels and peg board walls facilitate changing merchandise themes.

Visual Merchandise Presentation

Merchandise Presentation

"Merchandise presentation" has replaced the word "display" in retail talk. Why? Because it puts the emphasis back on merchandise, the core of retail.

One study on how men shop found that the main source of clothing ideas for men was window shopping. Another study from _Glamour_ magazine found that the store displays were the prime source of fashion ideas for women. An impressive window display of bestsellers, gift suggestions, and "what's new" can be a magnet into a store. So give this subject the attention it deserves, especially as it can cost next to nothing to set up.

Here's what retailers need to consider to improve visual merchandise presentation:

1. Support of selling strategy: how will merchandise presentation support either
    * full service_____
    * self-service _____
    * other_____?
2. Role of fixtures: what is the store's approach to visual impact given
    * the use of vertical space (the higher the fixture the more merchandise and sales per square foot)
    * the need for flexibility and signs?
3. Lighting: the need for highlights and drama
    * general or ambient
    * spots for merchandise features
4. Use of props: only as needed
    * appropriate to the concept and to the category (e.g., travel

props with books, cross-promotions with travel agencies, and magazines)

5. Merchandise presentation that integrates with advertising and promotion

Signs That Sell

Design for a productive store should include a formal plan of a three-tier signage system to help shoppers have an efficient, hassle-free experience. The system will have:

1. Higher-level, larger signs for:

- department identification (e.g., business, travel, cookbooks, and children's books)
- major ideas and services (e.g., special orders and gift wrapping)
- checkouts and service desk (e.g., vision statement and policies)
- major sales (e.g., back-to-school)

Shoppers can't miss this deal.

A great combination of product information and visual aids equal a silent salesperson.

2. Shop signs that are focused and hard-hitting:

- seasonal (e.g., Christmas)

- new products (e.g., What's new in technology)

- strong lines (e.g., "Our bestselling garden books")

- often graphics do a better job than words

3. Point-of-sale signs give purchasing information about:

- products

- price

- promotions

In-store signage should be used only if it:

- has an eye-catching heading, and/or

- tells a benefit-story.

The visual or merchandise presentation format must complement the level of sales service and be supported with:

Below, left:
Powerfully brings
product to life.

- advertising materials and posters

- audiovisuals

Below, right:
Great combination of
service and fashion
show.

- demonstrations, seminars, author signings, etc.

Organize Visual Merchandise Presentation

Productive retailers must bring their strongest efforts to bear at the point-of-sale. This is where strategic planning comes to fruition. It is the last 12 inches across the sales counter or the fixture shelves that makes the critical difference between a shopper who is "just looking" and one who is "buying."

The key elements in effective visual merchandise presentation are:
Departmentalize. Keep all assortments of each classification together for visual impact and shopping ease. Certainly you can accessorize one category with another, but strong parent departments and classifications must exist in order for the shopper to see easily and compare the full ranges of assortments. Let the dominance of the category show in the organization of the merchandise.

Very effective impact from color-blocking.

Tell a story about the store's merchandise strengths. If there are wide assortments, show them; if it is a single theme, demonstrate it; if there is a breadth or depth of focus, prove it by having the product always on hand.

Coordinated editing of color story.

The merchandise itself tells the story.

Hand dipping chocolates in the window. Great visual merchandising!

Let the merchandise make the statement and avoid excessive display props. Shoppers buy products, not fixtures and stands.

Keep fixtures, walls, windows, main traffic and fixtures flexible for the ever-changing flow of seasonal change and new trends in merchandise.

Identify bestsellers and isolate them with "mass with class" presentation. Feature ample product, and do it in an appealing way.

One hot item in a multitude of color choices.

Power Merchandising

Productive stores look productive. They have bestsellers mass merchandised at the entrance and shown in the windows. They have the right-hand entrance wall heavily stocked with the most profitable and sought-after categories and their end aisles or highly visible areas feature interesting, new items. The service desk is stacked with impulse items. These principles apply to all types of stores whether high-end or discount.

Power Merchandising

The proper implementation of power merchandising in a store can mean the difference between a 5% increase and a 15% increase; or a 38% and a 42% gross margin, respectively.

Smart, productive retailers believe in and work the *80/20 principle:* 80% of sales come from 20% of inventory. They know their Key Volume Items or KVIs, and power merchandise these items by following the three I's. (See page 69.)

Power merchandising is:

- Presenting lead or core categories in a prominent position in the store, often the main aisle or the first wall as customers enter the store.

- Buying proven items in depth, usually with expanded color, size and range to show off merchandise strengths.

- Mass-displaying lead items at key traffic points to send a "this merchandise is important" message to shoppers.

- Supporting key volume items with heavy repeat advertising, staff training, windows, and signs.

- Negotiating better buys based on your larger quantities.

Below, left:
Powerful presentation
can create a bestseller.

Below, right:
Simple and effective.
This moved a lot of
merchandise.

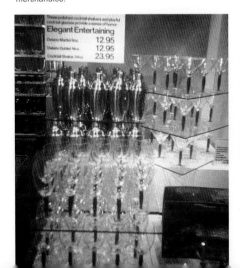

Power Aisles and Walls

The next step is to dramatically show off a store's merchandise strengths by building a power wall or aisle.

Power Walls and Aisles are a combination of:

- broad assortments
- value pricing, and
- clear layout and presentation.

When combining the three I's with an assertive visual presentation and pricing, the benefits can be impressive:

- Bookstores that feature bestsellers (top 10–20) and/or their key categories can generate +20% of total sales from 5% of their space.
- Drugstores with power walls of cosmetics, hair care, and beauty aids report big sales increases, and do 30% of store sales from 10% of store space.
- Hardware and do-it-yourself stores with power aisles devoted to seasonal specials in garden supplies, barbecues, Christmas decorations, and spring cleaning report 20% of store sales from 5% of space.
- Apparel stores that anchor their store with major presentations of jeans or sweats do 20% of sales in less than 5% of space. Tilley Endurables (travel and adventure wear specialists) does 12% of its store sales from just one item – their famous hat – from a power wall that is ± 2% of space and produces sales per foot of $2,500.

To build a power wall or aisle a retailer should:

- be prepared to spend up to a year to test and build assortments to build the department or classification,

- add mini power walls and aisles for second and third priorities, and

- drop unimportant or fringe subclassifications.

Power Wall Plan Key Classification Category	Present $ and % of Store Sales		Good Place to Locate and Build a Power Presentation	Potential $ and % of Store Sales	
	$	%		$	%
	$	%		$	%
	$	%		$	%
	$	%		$	%

Bring these plans forward when you review a store's layout and productivity.

These awesome assortments draw shopper traffic from a wide trade area.

Note:

While working with a shopping center retailer support program, we were asked to help a gift shop that was not doing well. On my first visit, the store had a pleasant appearance with ample merchandise. Sales associates and management were pleasant and efficient. So those factors were not causing the sales problems. Going into my professional shopper mode, I went through the process of buying a series of gift products. It was then that I discovered the cause: the store had all of the various products spread throughout the entire shop – from one end to the other, from high to low. At no time could a shopper assess or comprehend the entire assortment of any one category. Staff thought this "boutique" look was great, but shoppers were finding it inefficient and frustrating. When they rearranged the various product categories into logical groups, the merchandise power of their assortments was shown. Sales responded positively. Also, this regrouping of products uncovered areas where they thought they had good assortments, but didn't because this could not be seen in the "hodgepodge" approach to presentation.

7. Improving Productivity with Marketing

John Wanamaker, founder of the first U.S. department store, once stated, "Half of my advertising doesn't work. Unfortunately, I don't know which half." Today more than ever, the marketing, communications, and sales promotion world is increasingly complex. Yet what we do know is that effective marketing is one of the driving forces behind putting excitement back into retailing. More importantly, it helps build strong shopper relations and customers for life. Productive retailers know that there has been a fundamental shift in how to approach marketing and communication.

Definition of the New Communications

Traditional retail mass-market advertising is no longer very effective because it:

- is mostly characterized by price and item advertising.
- is nondifferentiated, boring, and demeaning in its creative look and message, and also difficult to distinguish one store's ad from another. It speaks to customers, but makes no attempt to involve them directly.
- has a different look and message for print, radio, TV, in-store, direct marketing, packaging, and special events communications, with little or no integration.
- has different approaches in different merchandise categories at different times of the year.
- makes no attempt to target, isolate, and/or focus on key customer segments, the most productive prospect.
- is price-driven, with no imagination, ideas, or innovation.
- has little sense of what's working or not, no accountability, and no understanding of return on investment.

New communications put a real emphasis on the following:

- Selling products, along with the basic customer benefits that makes the store unique.

- Focusing first on existing high-volume high-profit customers and getting them to shop more often for more of their needs, and then going after new prospects that fit their concept.

- Building campaigns that include everything from awareness and image advertising to in-store direct marketing, public relations, and special events.

- Using metaphors, icons, and symbols to create unique looks.

- Highlighting the store as a medium, creatively bringing their concepts to life, and adding fun, buzz and energy to the shopping experience (e.g., American Girl in Chicago and New York City and Toys"R" Us in Times Square).

If there is one common mistake made by retailers and shopping centers, it is not clearly articulating, focusing, and measuring results against a clear objective. When discussing marketing programs, the first question should be "What is your objective?"

Setting Marketing Objectives

It is important for stores to pick one key objective and focus on it, namely, to:

- build awareness of the store.

- create an understanding of the concept.

- build a liking and preference for the concept.

- turn preference into visits.

- turn visits into purchases.

- turn purchases into return visits and more purchases.

- create loyal customers.

Be sure the tenants' goal is specific and measurable. Wherever possible, it should be supported with dollar amounts and time frames. Without an objective, a retailer will have trouble being consistent in their choice of tactics or programs. Certainly a lot of money will be wasted.

The Right Advertising Strategy

Obviously, the right strategy will support the overall choice of one of the *Four E's* solutions. A strategy is a plan to achieve a key goal. It's usually based on:

- delivering a wanted benefit,
- doing it better than the main competition, and
- doing the usual in an *unusual way.*

Tenants' marketing programs should be reviewed against these strategic standards.

How Much to Spend

Most chains control the budgets at home or in regional offices, with a small amount allocated for local market needs. If there is a local budget, it may be taken up by the amount contracted in the lease for the center's marketing program. For many retailers, center marketing programs are a contentious issue. Marketing department must be responsible for spending (investing) tenants' marketing funds strategically (leading to a specific goal), with clear objectives, and a program that measures results in relation to mutually agreed on objectives. Team play demands this approach.

How Much Should Stores Spend on Advertising and Promotion?

Check off one of three. Put points in right-hand column, add up and refer to guidelines at the bottom of this chart.

1. Store location:

❑   high traffic . . . . .1 point

❑   average.. . . . . .2 points

❑   low .3 points

3. Amount of competition:

❑   few competitors . . . . .1 point

❑   average . . . . .2 points

❑   many . . . . .3 points

2. Store's awareness in the marketplace:

❑   high awareness . . . . .1 point

❑   average . . . . .2 points

❑   low .3 points

4. Store concept emphasizes price:

❑   little emphasis . . . . .1 point

❑   average . . . . .2 points

❑   high . . . . .3 points

Total Points _____

Guidelines:

4 points   – low end of guideline

8 points   – medium end of guideline

12 points   – high end of guideline

For Example:

If you arrive at 8 points and you are in the radio, TV, consumer electronic business, then you should probably stay with industry average and spend 3.3% of sales on advertising. If you are at 12 points you should think about spending higher than the average, perhaps around 3.7%. At 4 points you could go below average to around 3%.

Commodity or Class of Business	Average %	Commodity or Class of Business	Average %
Apparel and accessory stores	2.4	Home furnishing stores	5.4
Department Stores (All)	3.5	Men's wear stores	3.1
Discount stores	1.2-2.9	Women's clothing stores	2.6
Restaurants	2.3	Shoes	2.4

Shopping center management can help ensure that retailers' marketing budgets are well spent by ensuring that advertised items are clearly identified in the store—by making sure "as advertised" signs, trained staff, and extra inventory featured in prominent areas aren't lacking.

In-store Promotional Support Tools

Having decided upon which promotional activities to include in the plan, retailers next need to make a list of support tools for each type of event to give marketing communications additional leverage with customers.

A typical list of in-store promotional support tools includes:

- Windows
- Feature displays
- Seminars and demonstrations
- Activities and special events
- Interactive displays

- Contests
- Staff incentives
- Point-of-sale signing or POS
- As-advertised cappers
- Special price ticketing

Tenants should be encouraged to use these promotional tools to strengthen promotional messages (both their own and center events):

- Product demonstrations: consider running a 10-minute "how to" demonstrating a product's key features to customers, often paid for and done by the supplier.
- Color photos: show the end use and real benefits of the product or service being offered.
- Chalkboard signs: usually associated with clearances or value offering, it can also be used to recognize associates and customers or special classes (e.g., cooking demonstration, author reading, and "how to" classes).
- Parcel stuffers: for customers to take away. They can include an offer or bounce-back on a future purchase, or additional information on how to use and service their new purchase.

A Media Plan that Works

Shopping center management can help tenants become more productive by giving them guidelines in decision-making. Certainly, the center's marketing manager will have the tools, resources, and skill to offer ideas or data so that the stores can make the right decisions.

Retail Tenants' Media Plan

A Media Plan determines where and when advertising will appear. It should be prepared with these ten steps in mind:

1. Reconfirm the role of advertising and the goals it is to achieve.

2. Be specific in terms of sale and awareness goals.

3. Establish a media budget; take out administrative, creative, and production costs and deal only with media.

4. Reconfirm target customers, the trading area, and the media most relevant to their interests.

5. Relate media to sales needs – by week, month, season, and year.

6. Break out media and allocate to weekly events.

7. Identify and evaluate opportunities to mix media; list the strengths and weaknesses of each medium.

8. Choose a media plan that best suits the store needs and goals.

9. Establish the reach, frequency and cost per thousand goals with the help of your media reps or center marketing management.

10. Firm up plan versus budget dollars; and the advertising costs versus sales plan.

Media Choices (in addition to local radio and television)

Shopping Center Media:

- Flyers and circulars
- Seasonal catalogues
- Special events
- Video
- Shopping bags
- Windows of vacant stores
- Posters
- Outdoor signs

Shopping Publications:

- Merchant-owned
- Independent

Miscellaneous Periodicals:

- Local and community newspapers and publications
- Theater programs
- National magazines
- Timetables
- College and school publications
- Directories

Database/Direct Mail:

- Letters
- Envelope enclosures:
  i) Stuffers
  ii) Folders
- Circulars
- Postcards and mailing cards
- Self-mailing folders
- Broadsides
- Booklets and catalogues
- Metered postage messages

Miscellaneous Direct Media:

- Dodgers, handbills, circulars
- Reprints of newspaper advertisements
- Wrapping supplies, merchandise labels
- Package inserts
- Gift novelties

Outdoor Signs:

- Posters
- Painted bulletins
- Electric signs

Transit Cards:

- Car cards
- Station posters
- Bus cards

Miscellaneous Signs:

- Taxicab signs, truck signs, and posters
- Theater curtains, slides
- Movie shorts
- Street banners
- Skywriting and airplane trailers
- Kites, balloons, and blimps
- "Sandwich-man" signs
- Pedestrian benches
- Projections on clouds
- Movie theaters (pre-film)

Cable and Video:

- In-store video and interactive video

Telecommunications:

- Telemarketing

Cyber Communications:

- CD-ROM
- E-mail
- Internet/World Wide Web (WWW) home page
- Electronic Data Interchange (EDI)
- Online Service
- Electronic Bulletin Boards
- Interactive TV and Kiosks

Co-op Advertising and Vendor-Support Programs*   Marketing dollars are always in short supply; therefore tenants can make the most of this source of funds and event support. Retailers should be encouraged to be aggressive in getting co-op marketing funds from their suppliers or manufacturers. Why? Because the supplier budgets co-op funds in relation to what a store purchases – so if you don't ask for co-op support, you won't be given it. Keep in mind that it may be possible to get funds for more than just advertising. Ask about windows, contests, visual presentation, staff training, demonstration, and sampling. Using co-op dollars to advertise not only can lead to stronger relationships with your stores' suppliers but also can generate a lot more traffic in your center, increasing sales and profits. It's a win-win situation for everyone—the more product your stores sell, the more co-op dollars you receive.

A vendor-supported program is a way of obtaining special promotional funds from your stores' key vendors (beyond those already generated through co-op programs). These extra dollars can subsidize various special events or promotions. A vendor-supported program means sales of products over and above shipments to retailers. This means that your stores have the opportunity to increase their sales while offering your supplier higher product visibility and greater customer awareness. Best of all, your retailers can get this extra support when they have a need for special promotion – these programs make a welcome addition for grand openings, anniversary sales, new product introductions, test marketing or even the remodeling of a store. Once the supplier sees a need, the promotion can take place in your center or at a store – whichever is best for the type of promotion being held.

* This section adapted from pages 34-39 of ICSC's *Effective Newspaper Advertising for Shopping Centers.*

Where Does Co-op Money Come From?

Traditionally, co-op has three avenues of distribution:

1. Manufacturer to retailer—This is co-op money made available from the manufacturer to the retailer. This co-op is available regardless of whether the product is purchased from the manufacturer or from a distributor.

2. Manufacturer to distributor—Co-op funds are provided to the distributor and must be claimed through the distributor by the retailer.

3. Ingredient producer and end-product producer—Co-op funds are provided jointly by the manufacturer of an ingredient and the manufacturer of the end product.

Keep in mind that co-op dollars are only good during the year your stores earn them. So if they do not use them, they will lose them along with the potential for additional traffic created with additional newspaper advertising. Co-op dollars available to your stores should be incorporated into their advertising plan each year.

Merchant Participatory Budget Worksheet

Month	Percentage of Last Year Total Center Sales	x Current Year Total Ad Budget	= Monthly Ad Budget	Names and Dates of Merchant Participatory Events			
				Event	Date	Event	Date
January							
February							
March							
April							
May							
June							
July							
August							
September							
October							
November							
December							

Source: ICSC's The Library of Shopping Center Marketing Forms.

Merchant Participatory Advertising Recap

Event Name	Date	Type (Publication/Spots)	No. of Merchants Participating	$ Generated (# Merchants x Cost)	Cost to Center	Remarks/Future Recommendations

Source: ICSC's *The Library of Shopping Center Marketing Forms.*

What to Look for in a Co-op Plan:

A co-op plan contains five key elements, as follows:

1. Accrual—The amount of co-op money available to a retailer for advertising.

2. Participation or performance—The manufacturer's share of the cost of advertising. This can range from 20 percent to 100 percent.

3. Requirements from the manufacturer—The rules that the manufacturer sets up for its particular plan. All requirements must be met in order to qualify for co-op reimbursement.

4. Term or timing—The time period in which a particular co-op plan is in effect. Generally, the term is a calendar year.

5. Claim—The request for reimbursement to the manufacturer or distributor filed by the retailer or newspaper on the retailer's behalf.

The Six-Step Co-op Action Plan for Retailers

1. List your top 25 suppliers. They produce most of a retailer's business and will probably provide most of the co-op money available. And because the retailer already advertises their products, their co-op money will fit the retailer's ad budget most conveniently.

2. Get everything a retailer needs to know. Using the vendor's account number, your newspaper rep can determine all the important elements of a particular co-op program: (a) your retailer's co-op accrual level, (b) the time period involved, and (c) any special requirements.

3. Allocate co-op money. Divide each product's co-op dollars on a month-by-month basis consistent with monthly sales trends for the product category.

4. Integrate co-op into your retailer's ad plans. This will allow the retailer to plan for larger ads or more frequent ads for its most popular products in their best-selling seasons.

5. Create co-op ads that pull. A co-op ad should move merchandise, promote the retailer's image, and meet the requirements of the retailer's supplier. Your local newspaper can help your retailer prepare this type of ad.

6. Collect the co-op money due the retailer. The faster the retailer submits the claim package, the faster the retailer will be repaid by its supplier.

The following forms can help you administer your program:

Participatory Advertising Evaluation

1. Did you advertise in _____?
(event name and date)

If yes, please answer the following:

1a. Was your ad ❑ Image Advertising

❑ Merchandise Advertising

1b. What product(s) did you advertise in the event?

Item(s) _____   Price _____

Item(s) _____   Price _____

Item(s) _____   Price _____

Item(s) _____   Price _____

Item(s) _____   Price _____

1c. How many items were sold during this period? (Please note responses or increased traffic.)

_____

_____

_____

_____

2. What was your sales percentage increase or decrease for the following periods: _____ to _____

compared with last year's sales for these dates?

Overall Percentage Increase	Overall Percentage Decreased	Percentage Increased on Advertised Item	Percentage Decreased on Advertised Item
_____	_____	_____	_____
_____	_____	_____	_____
_____	_____	_____	_____
_____	_____	_____	_____
_____			

3. What improvements could be made to future cooperative events?

_____

_____

_____

_____

Source: ICSC's The Library of Shopping Center Marketing Forms.

Tenant Advertising

This form helps you determine your shopping center's buying power by listing the total advertising dollars spent by your center and each of your center's tenants in local print media. It will give you an idea of what your total budget power is for the upcoming budget year.

Center/Tenants	Current Print Advertising Budget for this Year	Projected Print Advertising Budget for Next Year
Center		
Tenants		
(Add pages to list additional tenants)		
Total		

Source: ICSC's Effective Newspaper Advertising for Shopping Centers.

8. Understanding Store Operations

There is probably no other business (with the exception of a large restaurant) that is more-complicated and demanding than retail. Hours are long to serve ever-more-demanding shoppers in a hypercompetitive marketplace. Retail management is bombarded continually with demands from a wide range of people with issues that need immediate attention. Some of these are outlined below.

Thousands of Different Consumers: 12+ Hours a Day, 362 Days a Year

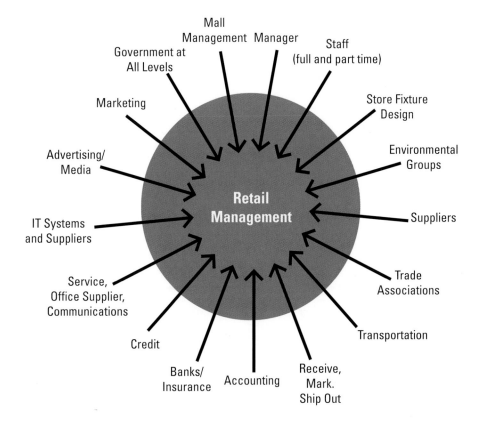

How Stores   Whether in large chains or a single store, most retailers are

Operate   organized into fairly distinct functions. These are:

CEO: Total responsibility
Operations: In-store activities and logistics
Merchandise: Vendor relationships and company inventory
Finance: Finance, accounting, controller
Business Process: IT, systems and logistics
Marketing: Brand, communication, events, customer
                              relationship management
Real Estate: Planning and construction
Non-store Retailing: Catalog and e-retail

With the exception of regional chains and independents, most stores
in your center report to a regional manager. This person likely will
have risen from the ranks of store manager within the region or
company. It is essential for center management to cultivate a close
working relationship with this level of retail management in order to
get the best store manager assigned to your center; get informed on
how much leeway the store has on making marketing, staffing, and
inventory decisions. Resolve any problems as quickly as possible;
and try to stand out among the many other centers that you are
competing with for resources.

The store manager is a critical position for both the center and its
tenants. Most chain store managers have limited control of inventory
assortments, timing of markdowns, physical layout, financials, and
business decisions. However, with improved technology and good
communication programs, chain stores are adapting inventory and
marketing to local markets better than in the past. You might inquire
whether or not the chain uses a price optimization or gross margin
enhancing software program.

The store manager's main task is finding the right key support management (two or more to cover days, hours, and holidays), plus good staff. If the long hours and many days of operation weren't enough, the low pay doesn't help keep staff for long. Not surprisingly, at the sales associate level, the industry's number one problem is turnover. On average, staff stay 60 days in fast food, and one home improvement chain reported its average turnover to be 180 days. This situation is obviously bad for the center's overall shopping experience. Just think of completing a year's great marketing campaign on what a wonderful place your center is to shop when more than half of the retail staff will be gone to other jobs! The second most important task for store managers is ensuring the myriad of small tasks (from housekeeping to shelf stocking to visual presentation) is completed by the staff at an excellent level.

Another "Catch 22" for both center and retail management is the days and hours of opening. Obviously, the longer you are open, the more sales you can do. But the more days and the longer the hours, the weaker the in-store staffing and quality of service tends to be.

Note:

Despite the scenarios described above, many stores have excellent staff and service. One popular chain has only 10% turnover because they pay fairly, have good benefits, do a lot of training, recognize excellent performance on a wide scale, have a "fun" culture, and in many different ways seek feedback and ideas. This result is a productive store and an industry leader in ROI and sales growth.

Sales Staff
Scheduling

While there are many ways of scheduling sales associates, the most common is outlined below. Whatever the process, the principles and goals are the same, namely to keep the cost of staff within the dollar or percentage plan while delivering good customer service.

Sales wages are planned in relation to net sales:

Sales Plan	$1,000,000
Total Wages	$100,000 or 10%, wage-to-sales ratio or percentage
Manager	$25,000
Sales Staff	$75,000

If sales drop significantly (e.g., 10% to $900,000), then it is likely the wage budget will be cut to $90,000 (less $25,000 for the manager and $65,000 for sales staff or a -13% decrease in the sales staff budget).

If sales go over the plan by 10% (e.g., $1,100,000), it is unlikely that the store would be allowed to add $10,000 to staffing, but a 15% increase should add dollars to the sales staff budget. However, this practice will vary from retailer to retailer.

Step 1: Yearly Wage Plan

The sales wage budget is allocated to each month with slow months (February and July) getting fewer dollars, but proportionately higher wage-to-sales percentages than the busy peak months (November and December).

	J	F	M	A	M	J	J	A	S	O	N	D
Sales	$70,000	$50,000	$60,000	$80,000	$80,000	$70,000	$60,000	$70,000	$100,000	$120,000	$150,000	$200,000
Budget	$ 7,000	$ 7,000	$ 7,000	$ 8,000	$ 8,000	$ 7,000	$ 7,000	$ 7,000	$ 9,000	$ 10,000	$ 10,000	$ 12,000
%	10%	7%	8.5%	10%	10%	10%	8.5%	10%	9%	8%	6.6%	6%

Step 2: Weekly Wage Plan

For each month, week, and day there should be a fixed number of staff in a store. Even for small stores, it is essential to have two people covering the floor. This is for service, security and shoplifting reasons.

Typically the schedule, plan, and budget are prepared on an hourly shift basis. The principles are as follows:

- Peak staff coverage in relation to center traffic peaks and store shopping visits.
- Schedule the best staff and managers for the busiest days.
- Balance experienced full-time staff with newer part-time staff.

Store Weekly Staff Schedule Plan

	Weekly Cost	M	T	W	T	F	S	S	Total
Sales Plan		$1,500	$2,000	$1,500	$2,000	$3,000	$6,000	$4,000	$20,000
Manager	$500		X	X	X	X	X		$ 500
Assistant Manager	$400	X			X	X	X	X	$ 400
Full-time (1)	$360	X	X	X			X	X	$ 360
Full-time (2)	$360		X	X	X	X	X		$ 360
Part-time (1)	$7/hour	½				½	X	X	$ 225
Part-time (2)	$7/hour	½	½	½				½	$ 112
Plan of 10% of sales or $2,000									**$1,956**

Step 3: The Daily Plan

The daily plan schedules the hours that staff work in relation to center and store traffic.

	Early Week	**Saturday**
AM		
10–12	Assistant Manager	Store Manager
	Part-time (1)	Full-time (1)
		Part-time (1)
PM		
12–2	Assistant Manager	Store Manager
	Full-time (1)	Full-time (1)
	Part-time (1)	Part-time (1)
2–6	Assistant Manager	Store Manager
	Full-time (1)	Assistant Manager
		Full-time (1)
		Part-time (2)
Evening		
6–9	Full-time (1)	Assistant Manager
	Part-time (2)	Full-time (2)

These are based on the assumption that both the store and the center measure traffic by quarter hour and use it as the basis of scheduling.

Retail Management Systems

Technology has become an integral part of retail business management. Today, affordable, off-the-shelf software packages are available that can provide even the smallest retailers with the same tools that until recently existed only in the domain of large retailers, which could justify the cost of custom-software solutions.

Integrated retail management systems create a competitive advantage by improving efficiency, reducing costs, increasing revenue and raising profitability. By collecting and integrating information from across the business and providing the means to effectively measure and report on performance, technology helps retailers continuously improve their operations.

What Are Retail Systems?

Shoppers have come to recognize retail technology and many have a superficial understanding of how they work. In many ways these systems are straightforward. The cash register processes sales and administers the various forms of tender, the scanner reads the UPC code on an item and matches it to an item file to determine the price and description. We have become comfortable with the function of debit/credit terminals and we know that security tags beep if they are not deactivated before leaving the store.

The appearance of retail hardware varies greatly from store to store. The look and feel of point-of-sale hardware has come to reflect the image of the retailer. Flat panel monitors imply innovation, forward thinking and high style. Keyboards and computers integrated into counters present an image of cleanliness, organization and clever design.

Regardless of physical differences, the purpose and function of retail hardware is fairly standard and can be summarized as follows:

- Registers/Customer Displays
- Debit/Credit Terminals
- Barcode Scanners
- Produce Scales
- Security Tag Deactivators/Detachers

It is important to recognize that software (more than the hardware) determines the overall value and potential of a retail management system.

Software Applications

Retail management software consists of interconnected components, or "modules," that vary depending on the sophistication of the package. There are several tiers of software targeting retailers of different sizes. In this section the various modules have been classified as either "Basic" (available in most off-the-shelf systems) or "Comprehensive" (usually confined to custom or large retailer applications). The more advanced functions are indicated below in italics.

a) Point of Sale (POS) Module

- Typical functions include:
  - Basic checkout functions, including sales and returns
  - Debit and credit authorization
  - Cash management
  - Reporting
  - Collection of customer information and administration of loyalty programs

b) Inventory Management

- Typical functions include:
  - Item definition - this includes basic measures like description, cost, retail price and UPC code
  - Purchasing
  - Receiving
  - Physical Inventory

– Price Management and Event Planning

– Forecasting tools to estimate sales and plan events

– Automated inventory replenishment

c) Accounting & Financials

Depending on the software package, this function can reside within the retail management system or can be handled by a separate accounting application. Regardless of the configuration, significant time savings and improved accuracy result when this system is linked to the POS application. The financial system is updated by the POS, thus eliminating considerable manual effort and reducing errors.

- Typical functions include:
  - General ledger
  - Accounts payable
  - Accounts receivable
  - Payroll / HR

d) Reporting Tools

All retail systems provide some degree of standard reporting and online inquiries. More advanced applications permit custom reporting. Accurate reporting of key business measures provides the foundation for management decisions.

e) Comprehensive System Modules

- E-Commerce integration
- Customer Relationship Management and loyalty application
- Plan-o-gramming and shelf layout
- Custom reporting

Trends and Innovations

The sophistication and capability of retail management systems have improved dramatically over the years and now several powerful new technologies will revolutionize the way retailers manage their stores and leverage their customer relationships. Typically, larger or innovative retailers are first to adopt the latest technology for competitive advantage. However, all retailers in your shopping center can benefit by keeping up with new technologies.

Wireless

WLANs

Wireless Local Area Networks (WLANs) are becoming increasingly popular among retailers because of the many benefits they provide. They allow for the use of connected handheld devices that improve employee productivity and customer service. WLANs also increase the flexibility of the POS by allowing registers to be placed where required. Some retailers are using Voice Over IP (VOIP) technology to provide in-store communications using the WLAN.

WiFi

"WiFi" refers to the creation of wireless internet access points - "hot spots" – for customer use. WiFi is used increasingly as a means of drawing customers into the retail environment and has mall-wide applications.

Radio Frequency Identification (RFID)

RFID is a wireless identification system that can track merchandise down to the unit level (e.g., from a specific can of tomato soup to a specific sweater).

The technology consists of two main components: (1) an RFID tag containing a microchip programmed with identifying information; and (2) an RFID Reader to collect the data from tags within a range of one to six feet.

RFID will greatly improve inventory accuracy by providing retailers with real-time inventory visibility throughout the supply chain. This helps retailers keep their shelves fully stocked and make it easy to find lost items in the store. It also helps preventing theft and fraud. For example, because each item is tracked when it is sold, it will not be possible for a customer to fraudulently return an item that was never actually purchased.

With multiple applications across numerous industries, costs are dropping rapidly. And fueled by a recent decision by Wal-Mart requiring RFID compliance from their top vendors by 2005, the technology is forecast to grow at a rate of more than 20% per year over the next five years.

Customer Relationship Management (CRM)

CRM is a hot topic for retailers today. Most major retailers engage in some degree of CRM. In fact, CRM is the main reason for the boom in loyalty cards and frequent buyer programs.

The key to CRM is gathering personal information about regular customers. Loyalty programs provide shoppers with an incentive to share their personal information. In turn, the retailer gathers and analyzes the shopping patterns of specific customers and customer segments in order to develop targeted marketing campaigns and product offerings that appeal to the retailer's best customers.

All of this analysis has a common purpose: identifying the best customers and maximizing their satisfaction in order to increase overall sales and profits.

Self Checkout

The concept of self checkout isn't new, but the execution has greatly improved over earlier versions. Self checkout is catching on all over the world – primarily in the grocery industry where customers welcome the opportunity to avoid waiting in checkout lines. Customers scan item bar codes and place items into their bags which are weighed throughout the process to deter theft. A single staff attendant can monitor multiple self-checkout lanes, greatly reducing labor costs.

Stored Value / Gift Cards

It seems like every major retailer is promoting gift cards – and for good reason! They are the perfect gift and a big improvement over paper gift certificates. For the retailer, they are easier to process and potentially very profitable (especially when cards are not redeemed). For the customer, gift cards are easier to handle and are more secure since they can be voided or re-issued easily. Gift cards also have no value until they are activated at the register, unlike certificates, which are pre-printed with values and are as good as cash if stolen.

Kiosks

Kiosks have proven to be valuable self-service tools for retailers. The number of applications is endless and includes:

- providing product information
- gathering survey information
- providing web access
- providing digital photo services

- gift registry
- in-store advance ordering (e.g., deli counter)

In the mall, kiosks can provide customers with directions and information about the services they are interested in, as well as to dispense specific coupons and offers. They can also be used to gather customer information through surveys or to administer mall loyalty programs.

Price Optimization

These applications use complex algorithms based on myriad factors to help retailers understand how best to price their products for a specific customer or market. They allow retailers to explore various scenarios such as the effect of price on unit sales and profit. Additional factors such as advertising are also considered in an effort to determine at what price are profits maximized.

The high cost of price optimization systems means that they will only be used by larger retailers. They're unlikely to be used by store personnel, but rather by head office management to figure out regional pricing strategies.

Center-wide Solutions

There are a number of technologies that have potential applications for your center as a whole. These include the use of kiosks and the provision of wireless hot spots. In the future, Electronic Article Surveillance (EAS) could be administered at the mall level when RFID becomes an industry standard practice. Individual stores would no longer need their own security systems since the location of specific items could be tracked throughout the mall.

Retailers that successfully apply technology to their business increase their value as tenants. So, as a shopping center manager, it is in your interest to encourage awareness about retail technology. Consider including a section about retail systems in your tenant newsletter. Perhaps a tenant committee could be formed to review new products. Retail system vendors and consultants can be valuable resources and many would welcome the opportunity to provide you with basic information.

Tips on Maximizing the Value of the Shopping Center Website

- Include links to the sites of your retailers.
- Place the center hours and directions on the home page.
- The center directory should provide links to a separate page for each store. Photos of the store help the customer visualize the shopping experience.
- Create a link for new stores.
- Provide marketing opportunities for your tenants to offset the costs of site maintenance.
- Tenants may also be interested in placing their specific job listings on the center site.
- A calendar of events can highlight additional reasons to visit the mall such as antique shows or performances. You can also use your website to allow event exhibitors to apply.
- Indicate the key retail holidays and the events surrounding them.
- Create links for the services that your center provides such as personal shopping assistance, bridal and gift registry, gift wrapping, valet parking, gift certificates, child care, etc.
- Provide center management information, leasing, employment, and contacts.
- Indicate the handicap accessibility of your shopping center.
- Provide a bit of history about the center including some historical pictures if you have any.
- It may be helpful to provide a list of frequently asked questions in order to provide miscellaneous information to customers.
- If your shopping center has a loyalty program, your site can be used for registration, which helps create a targeted mailing list.

9. Occupancy Costs in the Retail Model

Occupancy costs are of paramount concern to all retailers. This is because they are fixed for long periods of time, and, after wages (which are somewhat variable), they are the second largest expense. Many retailers will have net profits of just 2–5%, which means a miscalculation on location or store size or base rent will increase occupancy costs by just a few percentage points – and put the store at risk. In turn, this can lead to the decision not to invest or update the store, which creates a downward productivity spiral and a detriment to the center.

Beyond getting the best rental deal, centers are faced with several conflicting issues, namely:

- Can increases in short-term rent be reconciled with the need for considerable capital investments to keep your center relevant to changing customer needs?
- Are rents so high that tenant innovation is squelched?
- If your traditional shopping center is in a stagnant or post-mature industry situation, would lowering rents help to revitalize your center?

Market Rental Rates

Certainly rents are set at a negotiated, competitive rate of what the market will bear. But keep in mind the real impact of premium rental rates.

Within the shopping center industry, a performance gap has been created by the traditional regional shopping center segment as it increased rents to ever-higher levels. This situation is similar to that of traditional department stores, which kept raising their mark-ups and gross margins over the past several decades. By doing this they opened up enough gross margin room (more than 40%) for the low gross margin discounter (with margins under 25%) to move in and create a new, low-cost retail sector. The discounters, as we all know, have been eating the department stores' lunch.

A similar phenomenon has happened with traditional centers' rising rents, which have gone as high as $60–$150 net per square foot for some specialty stores. This has opened a gap for power centers to enter the scene and offer retailers a low rent alternative at $15 – $25 net per square foot. Again, the new formula has been a huge success – at the expense of traditional centers. The result is a relatively new retail hierarchy. Once again, this scenario is being altered by the appearance of Web-based retailers (e.g., Amazon.com) with no "retail" occupancy costs at all. Clearly, rental rates must be viewed within a larger context and how the leasing situation in your center relates to the total competitive scene within your center's trading area.

Factors in the Rental Financials

Leasing management should clearly understand the retailers' economics of occupancy. Beyond just thinking about the gross occupancy to net sales ratios, sophisticated retailers analyze this by (a) the commodity that the retailer is in (e.g., apparel, electronics, fast food, etc.), (b) the nature and source of the store's products, (c) the number and quality of similar stores, and (d) the uniqueness and draw of the store.

a.   Different commodities have different gross margins. Vast differences exist between the gross margins (net sales – cost of goods, markdowns, shrinkage, workroom, discounts) in your center. Computers, for example, have gross margins of about 15%; French fries and coffee enjoy margins of about 80%. An astute lease negotiator has these and other facts in hand when negotiating with a retailer.

b.   Regard each store in terms of its source of products. Beyond knowing category averages for gross margins and operating costs, lease negotiators should be aware if extra margin is created in the way the store's products are sourced. Sometimes retailers that develop and create their own products will have gross margins of 50% higher than the industry or category norms. For example, private brand silver jewelry can have a gross margin of 80% instead of the 50% norm for jewelry.

c.   Getting the right blend of retailers is both art and science. Your center should have a retail merchandise mix model that predicts revenues by store category group, location, area of the center, and square foot. Using this model, the impact of a specific store in a specific location can be analyzed. Armed with this information, center management can make astute decisions on location, clustering, mix, and rent rates, plus appropriate tenant incentives and performance and design standards.

d.   Factoring in the uniqueness and draw of a store into rental negotiations requires careful analysis. What is today's hot concept can quickly cool off or become oversaturated in a few years. Yes, there are certain stores that have track records of being able to impact a trade area. But these situations are few and far between. When calculating the optimal rent for both parties, the following issues must be considered:

- Sustained drawing power and sales growth of the tenant;
- Ability to attract complementary tenants;

- Possibility of cannibalization and other uses to replace the weakened tenants;
- A realistic estimate of the extra traffic and sales that the tenant will attract, and which tenants will benefit; and,
- Oversaturation of the trade area with more of these stores, and a decline in drawing power to your center.

How Much Can a Store Afford?

The total occupancy costs for traditional, high gross margin retailers should not exceed approximately 12%, plus marketing costs of sales, or 20% (plus marketing budget) of the retailer's gross margin. N.B.: Total occupancy costs include rent, utilities, real estate taxes, and common area. Marketing costs should be added as stores in shopping centers can incur lower marketing costs because of the traffic generated by the total center.

Average Gross Margin	Ideal Occupancy Cost	Occupancy Costs Not to Exceed	20% of G.M.
40 – 50% (e.g., typical store)	8 – 10%	12%	8 – 10%
50 – 60% (e.g., fast food)	10 – 12%	15%	10 – 12%
30 – 40% (e.g., hardware)	6 – 8%	10%	6 8%
30% (e.g., appliance)	4 – 5%	6%	6%
20% (e.g. food)	3%	5%	4%
8 – 10% (e.g., warehouse clubs)			1.6 – 2%

Obviously, a center's rent mix can be increased with more retailers that have high gross margins (or low product costs).

Summary Tenant Information Tables for U.S. Super Regional Shopping Centers by Retail Category

Tenant Classification	Number in Sample	Median GLA in Square Feet	Median Sales Per Square Foot	Median Rate of Percentage Rent	Median Total Rent per Square Foot	Median Common Area Charge per Square Foot	Median Property Taxes per Square Foot	Median Insurance per Square Foot	Median Total Charges per Square Foot	Median Total Charges as Percent of Sales
General merchandise	198	81,138	$158.68	2.50%	$4.45	$0.52	$0.92	$0.19	$5.60	4.13%
Food	332	980	361.12	7.50	39.75	8.14	3.13	0.25	58.76	16.22
Food Service	1,161	785	444.41	8.00	46.19	9.69	2.69	0.25	68.94	14.82
Clothing and accessories	2,339	3,378	316.35	6.00	26.00	7.91	3.33	0.25	42.78	13.35
Shoes	858	2,285	313.03	6.00	28.95	7.85	3.20	0.26	45.45	13.72
Home furnishings	263	3,069	300.24	6.00	28.00	8.18	3.61	0.24	44.12	14.53
Home appliances/music	437	2,520	354.57	5.00	26.00	7.74	2.70	0.26	41.72	10.84
Automotive	11	5,562	494.41	6.00	11.97	4.08	3.08		15.43	6.24
Hobby/special interest	471	2,474	272.21	6.00	25.00	7.50	2.72	0.24	40.32	13.40
Gifts/specialty	819	2,392	276.94	6.00	28.83	7.96	3.45	0.22	46.01	15.55
Jewelry	740	1,200	852.21	6.00	66.42	8.32	3.22	0.25	86.04	10.12
Drugs	25	9,645	232.87	3.00	15.00	6.88	2.22	0.21	29.64	11.27
Other retail	890	1,031	400.86	7.00	39.49	8.17	3.37	0.26	57.12	14.72
Personal services	646	1,122	294.17	7.00	30.00	7.90	2.88	0.25	46.70	15.00
Entertainment/community	135	4,048	68.19	10.00	14.57	4.69	1.76	0.18	21.07	28.85
Financial	111	300			75.00	7.23	1.67	0.07	84.30	
Offices (Other than Financial)	75	1,452	347.55	6.00	25.50	9.30	1.32	0.06	38.20	13.36

Source: *Dollars and Cents of Shopping Centers*, Urban Land Institute, © 2002. This material is reproduced with the permission of the Urban Land Institute.

For additional insight, the Urban Land Institute publication *Dollars and Cents of Shopping Centers* gives a good basic outline of costs. But beware, these are just guidelines; many centers exceed these figures.

Is This Store Operated to Create High Gross Margins?

Beyond developing awareness of gross margins by store category, a smart lease negotiator will learn to spot a store within the industry category that has extra gross margin and room to pay a bit more rent. For example, these two stores sell exactly the same category of merchandise, but have two very different pre-overhead and net profit situations:

Apparel Store	Store A	Store B
	National Brands and Name Designers	Private Brands, Own Designers, Imports
Sales	$2,000,000	$2,000,000
Gross Margin (40%)	$ 800,000	$ 800,000
Import Margin	$ 0	$ 400,000
Total Gross Margin	$ 800,000	$1,200,000
Expenses (35%)	$ 750,000	$ 750,000
Profit	$ 50,000	$ 450,000

Which type of store can you get more rent from? However, knowing that store B can pay more rent does not automatically lead to the fact that you will get more rent from it. Typically, stores (like B) that have developed their own private brands and supply programs are usually very sophisticated, have national brand status, and will be loath to give up in rent what they have created. In reality, their brand or store name may be powerful enough in the marketplace that they can actually negotiate a lower than normal lease rate. Obviously, there is an opportunity to get more rent from store B, and if the base rent cannot be raised, then a higher percentage rent should be sought.

What Is a Fair Rent?

Rents are a double-edged sword. Developers and landlords want long-term, sustained cash flow and appreciation. To get this, they need to have their center thrive in the tumultuous retail world, a world that changes with each season. This means creating an environment and experience where the retail-tenant mix is:

- relevant – with new market-sensitive services and stores;
- balanced – offering a combination of the market needs and center's role in the trade area;
- interesting and exciting – and an experience beyond just *shopping* and worth the trip; and,
- new and fresh – with something new to see, learn about, and to tell to others.

If this is what is needed for shopping center success, leases must state that retailers:

- meet high standards of design, service, and merchandising;
- continuously refresh, renew, or reinvent themselves;
- add specific dimensions to their store that involve extra-special and unique products, staff, services, and events; and,
- become unique and dominant in the marketplace.

The developer and investors have far too much vested in your shopping center to not take a proactive stance, especially if their long-term goals are to be realized.

Needless to say, the deal must fulfill the needs of both the center and the tenants. The center that (a) insists on the type of retailer described above, (b) strikes the rental rate that allows the retailer to have the funds to create this type of store, and (c) insists that any leeway (any amount less than the very maximum to be gained) in the rental amount is spent on store upgrading, will see sales rise significantly. The payback from this type of deal increases rental revenue, as well as both players' long-term stability.

The "right rent" should be fair enough to meet the landlord's required return on investment while giving the retailer space for a reasonable profit. This balanced formula must include the extra funds to create an exceptional experience for the shopper, which in turn will increase tha competitiveness and revenues of both the tenants and the center.

Will Creative Retailing and Leasing Raise Shopping Center Revenues?

All progressive industries such as pharmaceuticals, food processing, aerospace and IT have significant R&D budgets. Industries and businesses that are not continually generating new ideas, testing and modifying new concepts can't possibly stay current with target customers. Your center should have an R&D allowance for the development of new retail concepts.

The only way for mature shopping centers to effectively fight low-rent power centers, discounters, and e-retailers is to offer *excitement* – something that the low-rent centers can't do. By adding value to your center through quality of experience, you're equipping your center with the most effective weapon to fight the low-rent centers, and putting yourself ahead of your direct competition. Of course, this principle is true for power and other specialty centers, too. This question shouldn't be whether your center should plan and create change, but rather how it will transform and keep up with consumers' even more demanding needs.

10. Getting Tenant Mix Right!

There is just too much at stake in the development and operations of a shopping center to take anything but a very strategic, analytical, and professional approach to tenant mix. The retail world and fluid consumer marketplace are far too competitive not to.

From convenience centers and specialty and ethnic shops to lifestyle shopping centers, every retailer today is affected by the forces of change. These include more demanding shoppers, new retail formats, e-retail, global competitors, the new economy, de-regulation, and technology. What is more alarming than the change itself, however, is the *multitude* of forces that are bringing about change. North America is experiencing major shifts in the composition of its consumers with:

a. the huge boomer bulge starting to enter a period of lower product consumption;

b. major changes in ethnicity happening in many regions (e.g., Hispanics in California, Vietnamese in Texas, or Asians in Canada); and,

c. significant shifts in attitudes towards value, fashion, and the environment.

At the store level, e-retail has impacted many retailers, especially bookstores, travel agents, computer and electronics stores and clothing stores. Wal-Mart, dollar stores, and the value sector are experiencing robust growth while traditional department and many specialty stores have lost significant market share. The retail rule is clearly "innovate or die." Outside of shopping centers, many downtowns and neighborhoods have found new life, just as there are many viable niche shopping alternatives such as catalogues, airports, or special events. No one in our industry can afford to coast, even for a moment. And because shopping centers are the theater for most of retailing, this industry is front and center as these changing acts take the stage.

Progressive Leasing Thinking

In order to survive and grow in this ever-changing scene, shopping center executives must have a clear plan to appeal to a specific target market segment by being distinctly better at selling something these shoppers want. Obviously, this plan has goals of asset appreciation, strong cash flow, and consistent revenue growth that are the result of a clear market focus.

The key elements of your shopping center's strategy should be as follows:

- The center must identify and stake out an important role in the trade area, which must be defined in terms of both tenant mix (merchandise, services, food, entertainment, etc.) and the social aspects of its shopping experience within the community.
- The center's role must be unique enough to own the specific role it fills. See your role in relation to all types of competition, whether direct (e.g., power centers, e-retail) or indirect (e.g., spending time on other activities such as hobbies).
- The center must build a highly focused competitive advantage that can be branded.
- The culture within your organization must go beyond "bricks and mortar" and thrive on continuous change and upgrading of the entire center's experience. Again, understand that the real

risk is in not testing new ideas and quickly responding to consumers.

Centers without a strategic tenant-mix plan run the risk of missing their financial goals because leasing decisions will not be consistently focused in a direction that leads to success. The competitive model for retailers in Chapter 1 applies to your shopping center too.

Shopping Center Strategic Competitiveness

Okay situation	Good situation	Desirable situation
Adequate experience Tenants are satisfactory Shopped occasionally ➡	Some differentiation Good experience On shoppers' short list ➡	Clearly superior Exceptional tenants Dominates trade area Leader in shoppers' minds Start shopping trips here

Foundation for a Winning Tenant-Mix

Progressive shopping center developers will have a model they use to create the right tenant mix for a very successful center. The elements in this marketing and financial model should include:

a. Identification of key consumer segments (by demographics, attitudes, behavior, and potential purchasing);

b. Analysis of all types of competitors (by commodity, market segment apparel, quality, drawing and power performance);

c. A formula for creating the right mix of tenants both by commodity and within each commodity group (right amount of space, stores, location and adjacencies), plus the right balance between commodity or category groups;

d. A system for forecasting revenues based on the above (impact of getting it right); and,

e.   An awareness of societal trends that impact consumption and
shopping behaviors (e.g., a forward-looking, strategic mindset).

The Role of the Center

Within your trade area, the role of the center must be clearly
articulated. Because there are so many shopping alternatives today,
anything less than a clearly defined position will be confusing to
shoppers, who will seek alternatives that they understand better. By
having a tenant-mix model that takes management through the five
steps above, opportunities for identifying consumers' needs and
trade area shortfalls will help to bring to light where a center can
strengthen its role, and thereby gain and strengthen market share.
For example, is one ethnic group being neglected? Are the home and
related sectors underserved?

Include the following research, analysis, and decisions when
deciding what role the center will have:

1. Position by retail market price appeal

- Deluxe (e.g., Tiffany & Co., Neiman Marcus)
- Up-market (e.g., Nordstrom, Williams-Sonoma, Talbot's)
- Mid-market (e.g., Macy's, Best Buy)
- Down-market (e.g., Wal-Mart, Payless Shoe Source)

2. Position by focusing on a lifestyle

- Traditional (e.g., JC Penney, The Gap, Ralph Lauren)
- Contemporary (e.g., Crate & Barrel, Aldo, Club Monaco)
- Avant-Garde (e.g., bebe, Abercrombie)

3. Combine the two (1 & 2 above) to better define the role in a two-
dimensional matrix.

Matrix Positioning – Shopping Centers

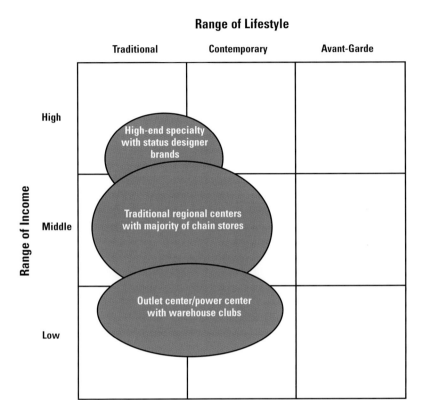

Range of Lifestyle

| | Traditional | Contemporary | Avant-Garde |

High-end specialty with status designer brands

Traditional regional centers with majority of chain stores

Outlet center/power center with warehouse clubs

Range of Income — High / Middle / Low

4. Include consideration of trade area peculiarities such as

- ethnicity
- age and family consumption
- higher education institutions
- unique competitors.

5. Decide on the true function or role.

Choose the Shopping Behavior on Which the Center Will Focus

Shopping Behavior	Center	Retailer	Social Factors
Fill replacement needs	• Convenience center • Neighborhood center	• Supermarket, drugstore, fast food	• Speed • Efficiency
Fill replacement needs and save money	• Warehouse clubs	• Price Club, Costco, Sam's Club	• Save money
Fill needs and some special purchases	• Community center	• Supermarket, bookstore, specialty food	• Efficiency
Fill wants, find personal expression products	• Traditional regional center	• Department and "fashion" specialty	• Ego, experience
Fill wants, save money	• Power centers	• Big box category killers	• Economy, efficiency
Fill special wants and give an experience	• Specialty centers • Lifestyle center	• Home, automotive • Pottery Barn • Designers	• Efficiency • Experience
Fill needs for social content	• Entertainment and lifestyle	• Theaters, restaurants, books	• A unique experience

Using Market Research for Reliable Trade Area Insights

The role of market research should be expanded to form the basis for a strategic tenant-mix and leasing plan. Using professional sample sizes, methodologies and questionnaires, the market research should give center management the following information:

- The trade area should be segmented primarily by lifestyle and secondly by demographics. The lifestyle segments are identified by their consumption behavior.
  - Traditional: eat basic foods like steaks and burgers; dress conservatively with low fashion awareness; social expression is not adventuresome.
  - Contemporary: try new trends; see themselves as fashionable; like going to new restaurants and movies.
  - Avant-Garde: reject other market segments; must have the newest fashions; test the very latest electronics; usually live in large urban centers.
- Define the number of people in each lifestyle segment and their approximated annual expenditures by commodity group. This will give center management an excellent snapshot of the trade area, as well as provide fact-based information on the size (i.e., dollar sales potential translated into square feet and number of stores) for each commodity's lifestyle and price group.
- Leasing management can then decide which retailers will fill the allotted spaces best.

Retail Audit

Progressive centers track current and proposed retailers closely. A database should organize this information:

- on maps that show all retailers in the trade area by location, which are color-coded by commodity. This information is very useful because it identifies clusters (strengths) of similar stores, as well as gaps (market opportunities) in commodities. (See sample.)

— by lists that can be cross-tabulated by district, commodity, lifestyle, and price zone appeal and size; plus estimates of store volume. This can be based on industry norms (e.g., 10,000 square feet x sales of $300 per square foot = $3,000,000).

— by likely new entrants to the center's trade area.

Social Trends

While individual centers will not likely track general social, attitudinal, and behavioral consumer trends, home offices should. The pace of change within shopping centers is often slow, due in part to five-, ten-, and more-year leases, and also due in part to traditional management practices; therefore, it is critical that shopping center leaders keep information and plans ahead of the curve. This information comes from a wide range of academic and professional research and consulting sources, as well as general media. Leading companies and centers disseminate this widely to their management.

Creating a Unique Tenant-Mix Strategy

Highly successful shopping centers focus on excelling at something important to target market shoppers and avoid trying to be all things to all people.

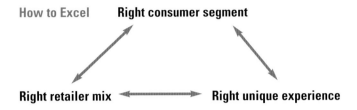

The best strategic model for a highly productive center will be based on a shopping experience that gives consumers what they want. While this is stating the obvious, it has not always been the practice of traditional shopping centers. Too often choosing and locating specialty stores in the centers is based on center-centric, rather than shopper-centric reasons. Stores are often located in a widely dispersed pattern to force shoppers to cover the entire center with not enough thought on how to build adjacencies.

In prosperous cities, retail mix forms on its own without the "guidance" of leasing experts. Healthy, prosperous cities such as Manhattan, Seattle, Chicago, San Francisco and Toronto have many distinct downtown retail districts or nodes that have formed naturally, based on the lifestyle, not commodity, characteristics of the market they serve – and secondarily by other demographic features such as income. People congregate and shop based on how they live their lives. Retailers take their cue and move in. Take Manhattan as an example. This city's retail has developed as follows:

District Examples	Lifestyle Appeal	Income Appeal	Stores
Fifth Avenue	Traditional	Middle (and Upper)	The Gap, H & M, Saks
Upper Madison Avenue	Traditional	Upper	Designers and antiques
Lower Broadway	Contemporary	Middle	Designers, Cafes
Soho	Avant-Garde	Full Range	Prada, Kate Spade, galleries

Within these lifestyle districts, subgroupings of commodity strengths emerge, such as home and apparel stores and restaurants.

Progressive shopping centers should take a lifestyle approach to creating a tenant-mix strategy.* This means that the idea of a lifestyle center should be applied to all large regional, power, and specialty shopping centers. Within the center, clearly defined retail lifestyle streets or districts will help this natural strategy. Each unique lifestyle-distinct area within the center should have the following components:

- Lifestyle anchors like Macy's or Sears (mid-market traditional), Barney's (upmarket contemporary), Wal-Mart (down market traditional)
- Lifestyle specialty stores (i.e., group all traditional apparel stores or all contemporary specialty stores together)
- Lifestyle food courts with one food court per lifestyle group. For example, McDonald's and similar basic brands in the traditional or down-market area, and the latest food trends in the contemporary area.
- Lifestyle services (e.g., two distinctly different personal service districts for the various ranges of beauty, spas, and financial institutions).
- Décor, music, common area seating, unique washrooms, and staff that mirror the lifestyle of the various target shopper segments in each lifestyle district or neighborhood of the center.

Does this mean that people will be less likely to shop the entire center? Yes. But the old-school strategy to force shoppers to walk the entire center to comparison shop is counterproductive. Two

---

* See Appendix B: Rethinking the Regional Shopping Center Layout.

things will happen:

1. Shoppers will leave and find a more efficient way.

2. Shoppers will "laser-beam" shop; they'll park near the store they want to visit and get in and out as fast as they can. And miss many stores that they would have otherwise been exposed to if they were clustered together in a complementary lifestyle group.

This approach to tenant mix takes the center to a new experience level and offers shoppers "their place" to visit, shop, and even hang out. This results in consumers coming more often and spending more time in your center. The revenue results are obvious.

One alternative to clustering stores by lifestyle groups is to cluster by product group. Yet, while this has a logical ring to it — "it will be easier to shop and compare" — in reality, it doesn't pan out that way. People shop in stores they relate to and don't necessarily comparison shop in stores that don't reflect their self-image – even if that shop is next door. Impulse shopping, for instance, happens when stores are clustered by lifestyle, not product type.

Note:

We know of two centers that tried clustering like retailers together. One in Los Angeles clustered men's wear and another in Toronto clustered children's wear, plus appropriate entertainment. In both cases, sales increases were not forthcoming. The mix of very traditional to very avant-garde shops with a wide range of price points did not add up to meaningful critical mass in the shoppers' eyes. And as time went on, these clusters were abandoned.

Getting Your   Within the controlled environment of your center, you have the
Retail Mix Right   opportunity to plan the ideal balance of stores – both between and
                        within product or commodity gaps. These decisions should be guided
                        by the general strategic framework you have chosen on pages
                        133–136, namely:

- Your center's unique role vis-à-vis the trade area and
  competition (e.g., the top-of-mind destinations for personal
  expression products and services)
- Retail and product groups that are over or underserved (e.g.,
  extra space and specialty shops in home, gifts, and cafés)
- Opportunities to add an extra dimension and experience to your
  center (e.g., special food and new service courts).

Inter-commodity Balance

Market research will help to confirm the right strategic direction
along with the ideal mix of space and number of stores to plan for
each commodity or product group. These must be well balanced by
lifestyle and pricing. Too often we have observed shopping centers
with a poorly balanced mix of stores among complementary
commodity groups. For example, the center on page 143 has a dual
problem of improper balance with women's sports and casual wear
and a shortage of shoe stores, thus forcing the contemporary apparel
shopper to go elsewhere for casual footwear, and under-serving the
large, traditional apparel market.

Example of Poor Balance in Tenant Mix Between Complementary Commodities/Categories

The Number of Stores in Each Lifestyle and Price Zone

Women's Casual Apparel

Range of Lifestyle

Price Zone	Traditional (60% of market)	Contemporary (35% of market)	Avant-Garde (5% of market)
High	2	1	0
Middle	4	8	1
Low	4	2	0

Women's Casual Shoes

Range of Lifestyle

Price Zone	Traditional (60% of market)	Contemporary (35% of market)	Avant-Garde (5% of market)
High	1	1	
Middle	4	1	
Low	2		

Note:

Observations: Women's Casual Apparel

- Traditional middle price market is under-assorted
- Contemporary market is over-assorted

Observations: Women's Casual Footwear

- Contemporary footwear is very weak, especially in relation to apparel

By balancing the space and number of stores between lifestyle and commodity groups the center will be become known as a one-stop shopping destination. As well, the design team can be directed by a market driven program, rather than having the leasing team "fill the spaces" as laid out by the architects.

How Many of Which Stores?

Deciding Tenant Mix and Choosing Retailers

Step 1: Cover the Basics

For each product, commodity or category, be sure that the basics are well covered for every lifestyle and income segment. Your mall likely needs just one store — the very best — to do this. How many stores are needed to cover the basic jeans or kakis segment? Just one or two.

Step 2: Plan to Dominate the Market

Determine the number of stores needed to be the market leader in each commodity lifestyle and price group that you have decided will

be a foundation of your center's role and strategic strength. Analyze the market potential in your trade area, deduct market share owned by competitors, and then add extra share of market that your center will gain from your superior strategy. Next, allocate square footage to each commodity lifestyle and price group. Then determine the number of stores this space would allow –- ensuring that the number of stores fulfills your strategic plans for uniqueness and dominance.

Step 3: Choosing the Right Stores

Your center needs both the right number and the right type of stores. If building dominance in women's or men's casual apparel and related products is your strategy, then the center's tenant mix must offer shoppers a choice of stores that avoids exact duplication. Ideally, a center should have the biggest and best assortment of high-quality retailers that are similar, but not identical. This gives shoppers an interesting variety of choice and the retailers a "monopoly" on their own market penetration. It also gives the center leverage when negotiating rents.

One way to look at the various positions of retailers is to view them in a "continuum of fashion appeal" with conservative or traditional at one end of the scale and avant-garde at the other.

Women's Apparel Fashion Appeal Continuum: For example

Traditional ━━━▶		Contemporary ━━━▶			Avant-Garde
Apparel:	Lands' End,	JCPenney,	Limited,	H&M,	Zara,	Hot Topic
Food:	McDonald's,	Steak Escape,	The Cheesecake Factory,			Wolfgang Puck

Within each fashion or lifestyle group, it is more appealing to shoppers to have complementary and adjacent retailers than a lot of very similar stores overlapping. Too many similar stores in each lifestyle commodity group creates a boring experience, as well as divides a market segment's potential, rather than attracting a greater range and number of shoppers.

Note:

A large shopping center developer was puzzled because although the facilities were new, the market was well-off, the tenants were desirable, and the ratio of women's apparel (the key problem commodity) to total center space was where it should be (35%, at that time) one of their centers was underperforming. In analyzing the tenant mix of the women's apparel group, it turned out that they had six jeans stores (moderate price, traditional sector) because the center management wanted to appeal to the large college market within their trade area. In over-covering the jeans category, the center did a poor job on traditional/middle price apparel for the non-student market. By neglecting the middle-income female, both the apparel stores and the center missed out on the buying power of this big-spending segment.

Increasing Financial Returns

The strategic approach to planning the right tenant mix will increase rental rates and long-term revenue because:

- Leasing will be more focused and command higher rents;

- People will stay longer, cross-shop more, return frequently, and drive up retail revenues;

- Marketing can be highly focused on specific target market segments;

- Your center, with 3–4 mini-lifestyle districts, will be a much more interesting and competitive shopping experience;

- There will be less tenant turnover; and

- The center will be a competitive alternative to both traditional and new shopping formats.

The Need for Getting Retail Right

The pressures on both shopping center and retail management have never been greater. This comes from the influence of the stock market, real estate investment trusts, pension funds, and financial institutions. Additional competition from direct (e-retail or catalogs) and indirect (new ways to spend leisure time) alternatives, plus a feisty consumer market raise the stakes in the shopping center industry. This is being played out in an economic climate where retail sales will not likely be as robust as they were in the past two decades. Already, North America has witnessed the dramatic decline in the number of shopping centers being built every year. Consequently, both centers and retailers will have to put greater emphasis on getting required revenue increases from improved center and store productivity. This marketing tactic requires increased emphasis on (a) improving your center's drawing power by creating a unique experience and (b) improving conversion rates on

getting shoppers or browsers to become buyers in your center.

This challenge is simply too demanding for your center management or retailers to go it alone: only by jointly revitalizing your center's shopping experience will you both survive and thrive.

Appendix A:

Top 200 Global Retailers

DT Rank 2003	Country of Origin	Name of Company	Formats	2002 Group Sales* (US$mil) e = estimate	2002 Retail sales (US$mil) e = estimate	2002 Group Income/ (Loss)* (US$mil)	Countries of Operations	5 yr. Retail Sales CAGR% (Local Currency)	5 yr. Net Income CAGR% (Local Currency)
1	US	Wal-Mart	Discount, Hypermarket, Supermarket, Superstore, Warehouse	244,524	229,617	8,039	Argentina, Brazil, Canada, China, Germany, Japan, South Korea, Mexico, Puerto Rico, UK, US	14.2%	17.9%
2	France	Carrefour	Cash & Carry, Convenience, Discount, Hypermarket, Specialty, Supermarket	65,011	65,011	1,314	Argentina, Belgium, Brazil, Chile, China, Columbia, Czech Rep., Dominican Republic, Egypt, France, Greece, Indonesia, Italy, Japan, Malaysia, Mexico, Oman, Poland, Portugal, Qatar, Romania, Singapore, Slovakia, Spain, S. Korea, Switzerland, Taiwan, Thailand, Tunisia, Turkey, UAE	18.7%	20.5%
3	US	Home Depot	DIY, Specialty	58,247	58,247	3,664	Canada, Mexico, Puerto Rico, US	19.2%	25.9%
4	US	Kroger	Convenience, Discount, Specialty, Supermarket, Warehouse	51,760	51,760	1,205	US	14.3%	23.9%
5	Germany	Metro	Cash & Carry, Department, DIY, Hypermarket, Specialty, Superstore	48,738	48,349	475	Austria, Belgium, Bulgaria, China, Croatia, Czech Rep., Denmark, France, Germany, Greece, Hungary, Italy, Japan, Luxembourg, Morocco, Netherlands, Poland, Portugal, Romania, Russia, Slovakia, Spain, Switzerland, Turkey, UK, Vietnam	12.4%	9.6%
6	US	Target	Department, Discount, Superstore	43,917	42,722	1,654	US	9.0%	17.1%
7	Netherlands	Ahold	Cash & Carry, Convenience, Discount, Drug, Hypermarket, Specialty, Supermarket	59,292	40,755	(1,143)	Argentina, Brazil, Chile, Costa Rica, Czech Rep., Denmark, Ecuador, El Salvador, Estonia, Guatemala, Honduras, Indonesia, Latvia, Lithuania, Malaysia, Netherlands, Nicaragua, Norway, Paraguay, Peru, Poland, Portugal, Slovakia, Spain, Sweden, Thailand, US	12.5%	NM
8	UK	Tesco	Convenience, Department, Hypermarket, Supermarket, Superstore	40,394	40,071	1,451	Czech Rep., Hungary, Rep. of Ireland, Malaysia, Poland, S. Korea, Slovakia, Taiwan, Thailand, UK	9.7%	13.4%

DT Rank 2003	Country of Origin	Name of Company	Formats	2002 Group Sales* (US$mil) e = estimate	2002 Retail sales (US $mil) e = estimate	2002 Group Income/ (Loss)* (US $mil)	Countries of Operations	5 yr. Retail Sales CAGR% (Local Currency)	5 yr. Net Income CAGR% (Local Currency)
9	US	Costco	Warehouse	37,993	37,993	700	Canada, Japan, S. Korea, Mexico, Puerto Rico, Taiwan, UK, US	9.8%	72.4%
10	US	Sears	Department, Mail Order, Specialty, e-commerce	41,366	35,698	1,376	Canada, Puerto Rico, US	-2.9%	3.0%
11	US	Albertsons	Drug, Supermarket, Warehouse	35,626	35,626	485	US	19.4%	-1.3%
12	Germany	Aldi Einkauf	Discount, Supermarket	e 33,837	e 33,837	n/a	Australia, Austria, Belgium, Denmark, France, Germany, Luxemburg, Netherlands, Rep. of Ireland, Spain, UK, US	15.2%	n/a
13	US	Safeway, Inc	Supermarket	32,399	32,399	(828)	Canada, Mexico, US	7.6%	NM
14	US	JCPenney	Department, Drug, Mail Order	32,347	32,347	405	Brazil, Puerto Rico, US	1.8%	-6.5%
15	France	Intermarché	Cash & Carry, Convenience, Discount, DIY, Food Service, Specialty, Supermarket, Superstore	e 31,688	e 31,688	n/a	Belgium, France, Germany, Poland, Portugal, Romania, Spain	9.2%	n/a
16	Germany	Rewe	Cash & Carry, Discount, DIY, Drug, Hypermarket, Specialty, Supermarket, Superstore	35,405	31,404	n/a	Austria, Bulgaria, Croatia, Czech Rep., France, Germany, Hungary, Italy, Poland, Romania, Slovakia, Ukraine	7.4%	n/a
17	US	Kmart	Discount, Superstore	30,762	30,762	(3,219)	US	-0.9%	NM
18	US	Walgreens	Drug	28,681	28,681	1,019	US, Puerto Rico	16.5%	18.5%
19	Germany	Edeka/AVA	Cash & Carry, Discount, DIY, Supermarket, Hypermarket, Superstore	e 27,166	e 26,514	n/a	Austria, Czech Rep., Denmark, France, Germany, Poland	17.2%	n/a
20	US	Lowe's	DIY	26,491	26,491	1,471	US	21.2%	32.7%
21	UK	J Sainsbury	Convenience, Hypermarket, Supermarket, Superstore	26,968	26,460	702	UK, US	3.5%	-1.4%

DT Rank 2003	Country of Origin	Name of Company	Formats	2002 Group Sales* (US$mil)	e = estimate	2002 Retail sales (US$mil)	e = estimate	2002 Group Income/ (Loss)* (US$mil)	Countries of Operations	5 yr. Retail Sales CAGR% (Local Currency)	5 yr. Net Income CAGR% (Local Currency)
22	Japan	Ito-Yokado	Convenience, Department, Food Service, Specialty, Supermarket, Superstore	27,245		26,179		171	Australia, China, Denmark, Guam, Japan, Malaysia, Mexico, Norway, Philippines, Puerto Rico, Singapore, S. Korea, Spain, Sweden, Taiwan, Thailand, Turkey, US	1.3%	-21.5%
23	France	Auchan	Department, Hypermarket, Specialty, Supermarket	26,071		26,071		276	Angola, Argentina, China, France, Hungary, Italy, Luxembourg, Mexico, Morocco, Poland, Portugal, Russia, Spain, Taiwan, US	4.2%	n/a
24	US	CVS	Drug	24,182		24,182		717	US	13.7%	79.9%
25	Germany	Tengelmann	Cash & Carry, Discount, DIY, Drug, Hypermarket, Specialty, Supermarket, Superstore	23,209	e	23,209	e	n/a	Austria, Canada, China, Czech Rep, Germany, Hungary, Italy, Poland, Portugal, Slovakia, Slovenia, Spain, Switzerland, US	-0.7%	n/a
26	Japan	Aeon	Convenience, DIY, Drug, Department, Discount, Food Service, Specialty, Supermarket, Superstore	25,155		23,030		418	Canada, China, Hong Kong, Japan, Malaysia, Thailand, UK, US	4.9%	35.4%
27	France	E Leclerc	Convenience, Hypermarket, Supermarket	22,229	e	22,229	e	n/a	France, Italy, Poland, Portugal, Slovenia, Spain	1.2%	n/a
28	Germany	Ldl & Schwarz	Cash & Carry, Discount, Hypermarket, Superstore	21,728	e	21,728	e	n/a	Austria, Belgium, Croatia, Czech Republic, Finland, France, Germany, Greece, Rep. of Ireland, Italy, Netherlands, Poland, Portugal, Slovakia, Spain, UK	14.8%	n/a
29	France	Casino	Cash & Carry, Convenience, Department, Discount, Food Service, Hypermarket, Specialty, Supermarket, Warehouse	21,620		21,620		n/a	Argentina, Bahrain, Belgium, Brazil, Colombia, Comoros, France, Lebanon, Madagascar, Mauritius, Mexico, Netherlands, Poland, Reunion, Taiwan, Thailand, Tunisia, Uruguay, US, Venezuela, Vietnam	14.5%	21.2%
30	US	Best Buy	Specialty	20,946		20,946		99	US	20.2%	1.0%

DT Rank 2003	Country of Origin	Name of Company	Formats	2002 Group Sales* (US$mil) e = estimate	2002 Retail sales (US $mil) e = estimate	2002 Group Income/ (Loss)* (US $mil)	Countries of Operations	5 yr. Retail Sales CAGR% (Local Currency)	5 yr. Net Income CAGR% (Local Currency)
31	Belgium	Delhaize Group	Cash & Carry, Convenience, Drug, Specialty, Supermarket	19,569	19,569	168	Belgium, Czech Rep., Greece, Indonesia, Luxembourg, Romania, Singapore, Slovakia, Thailand, US	10.4%	7.8%
32	UK	Kingfisher	DIY, Specialty	16,295	16,185	412	Belgium, Brazil, Canada, China, Czech Republic, France, Germany, Rep. Of Ireland, Italy, Luxembourg, Netherlands, Poland, Slovakia, Taiwan, Turkey, UK	11.0%	-6.9%
33	US	Publix	Convenience, Supermarket	15,931	15,931	632	US	7.3%	12.2%
34	US	Rite Aid	Drug	15,801	15,801	(112)	US	6.8%	NM
35	US	Federated Department Stores	Department, Mail Order	15,435	15,435	818	US	-0.3%	8.8%
36	US	McDonald's	Food Service	15,406	15,406	893	Global	6.2%	-11.5%
37	Australia	Woolworths	Convenience, Department, Specialty, Supermarket	15,389	15,225	356	Australia, New Zealand	9.1%	16.9%
38	Japan	Daiei	Department, Discount, Specialty, Supermarket, Superstore	17,910	14,941	1,103	China, Japan, US (Hawaii)	-7.7%	156.8%
39	Germany	KarstadtQuelle	Department, Mail Order, Specialty, e-commerce	14,959	14,724	153	Austria, Belgium, Bosnia-Herzogovina, Croatia, Czech Rep., Denmark, Finland, France, Germany, Hungary, Italy, Japan, Netherlands, Poland, Portugal, Slovakia, Slovenia, Spain, Sweden, Switzerland, UK, US	-3.1%	5.5%
40	US	Gap	Specialty	14,455	14,455	477	Canada, France, Germany, Japan, UK, US	17.3%	-2.2%
41	Australia	Coles Myer	Department, Specialty, Supermarket	13,560	13,560	187	Australia, New Zealand	4.5%	-0.8%
42	US	May Department Stores	Department, Specialty	13,491	13,491	542	US	1.8%	-6.9%

DT Rank 2003	Country of Origin	Name of Company	Formats	2002 Group Sales* (US$mil) [e = estimate]	2002 Retail sales (US$mil) [e = estimate]	2002 Group Income/(Loss)* (US$mil)	Countries of Operations	5 yr. Retail Sales CAGR% (Local Currency)	5 yr. Net Income CAGR% (Local Currency)
43	US	AutoNation	Auto	19,479	13,463 e	382	US	n/a	n/a
44	UK	Safeway	Convenience, Hypermarket, Supermarket, Superstore	13,366	13,366	260	UK	4.4%	-6.6%
45	Germany	Otto	Cash & Carry, Mail Order, Specialty, e-commerce	19,753	13,018	128	Austria, Belgium, China, Czech Rep., Denmark, France, Germany, Hungary, Italy, Japan, Korea, Netherlands, Norway, Poland, Portugal, Romania, Spain, Switzerland, Taiwan, UK, US	-2.6%	-9.4%
46	US	Winn-Dixie	Supermarket	12,168	12,168	239	Bahamas, US	-1.6%	3.2%
47	US	Meijer	Superstore	12,000	12,000 e	n/a	US	12.7%	n/a
48	UK	Marks and Spencer	Department, Specialty, Supermarket	12,497	11,986	743	Bahrain, Belgium, Bermuda, China, Croatia, Cyprus, Czech Rep., Finland, France, Germany, Greece, Hong Kong SAR, Hungary, India, Indonesia, Japan, Kuwait, Lebanon, Luxembourg, Malaysia, Malta, Netherlands, Philippines, Poland, Portugal, Qatar, Rep. of Ireland, Romania, Saudi Arabia, Singapore, Slovenia, South Korea, Spain, Taiwan, Thailand, Turkey, UAE, UK, US	-0.6%	-10.4%
49	US	TJX Cos.	Department, Specialty	11,981	11,981	578	Canada, Rep. of Ireland, UK, US	10.1%	13.6%
50	France	Pinault-Printemps-Redoute	Department, Mail Order, Specialty	25,894	11,410	1,503	Belgium, Brazil, Denmark, Estonia, Finland, France, Germany, Luxembourg, Norway, Portugal, Spain, Sweden, Switzerland, Taiwan, UK, US	12.0%	29.6%
51	US	Toys 'R' Us	Specialty	11,305	11,305	229	Australia, Austria, Bahrain, Canada, Denmark, Egypt, France, Germany, Hong Kong SAR, Indonesia, Israel, Japan, Kuwait, Malaysia, Mauritius, Netherlands, Norway, Portugal, Qatar, Saudi Arabia, Singapore, South Africa, Spain, Sweden, Switzerland, Taiwan, Turkey, UAE, UK, US	0.5%	-14.1%

DT Rank 2003	Country of Origin	Name of Company	Formats	2002 Group Sales* (US$mil) e = estimate	2002 Retail sales (US$mil) e = estimate	2002 Group Income/ (Loss)* (US$mil)	Countries of Operations	5 yr. Retail Sales CAGR% (Local Currency)	5 yr. Net Income CAGR% (Local Currency)
52	Spain	El Corte Ingles	Convenience, Department, Hypermarket, Specialty, Supermarket	12,701	10,910	520	Portugal, Spain	14.8%	24.7%
53	Canada	Loblaw	Convenience, Hypermarket, Supermarket, Superstore, Warehouse	14,709	10,900	464	Canada	9.2%	27.9%
54	Sweden	IKEA	Specialty	10,033	10,033	n/a	Australia, Austria, Belgium, Canada, China, Czech Rep., Denmark, Finland, France, Germany, Greece, Hong Kong SAR, Hungary, Iceland, Israel, Italy, Japan, Kuwait, Malaysia, Netherlands, Norway, Poland, Russia, Saudi Arabia, Singapore, Slovakia, Spain, Sweden, Switzerland, Taiwan, UAE, UK, US	15.0%	n/a
55	US	Circuit City	Auto, Specialty	9,954	9,954	106	US	4.5%	0.4%
56	US	SuperValu	Discount, Hypermarket, Supermarket, Superstore	19,160	9,848	257	US	15.1%	2.2%
57	Switzerland	Migros Genossenschaft	Convenience, Department, Hypermarket, Specialty, Supermarket, Superstore	13,022	9,844	115	France, Germany, Switzerland	2.4%	-8.5%
58	Japan	Uny	Convenience, Department, DIY, Drug, Specialty, Supermarket, Superstore	9,616	9,505	102	Hong Kong SAR, Japan	2.2%	-0.5%
59	France	Louis Delhaize	Cash & Carry, Convenience, Discount, Hypermarket, Specialty, Supermarket	9,497 e	9,497 e	n/a	Belgium, Guyana, France, Hungary, Luxembourg, Romania	5.4%	n/a
60	US	H.E. Butt	Supermarket	9,300 e	9,300 e	n/a	US, Mexico	7.7%	n/a
61	UK	Great Universal Stores	DIY, Mail Order, Specialty	11,056	9,141	388	Botswana, France, Germany, Lesotho, Namibia, Netherlands, Rep. of Ireland, Japan, Spain, South Africa, Sweden, Swaziland, UK, US	18.6%	-10.4%

DT Rank 2003	Country of Origin	Name of Company	2002 Group Sales (US$mil) e = estimate	2002 Retail sales (US$mil) e = estimate	2002 Group Income/(Loss)* (US $mil)	Countries of Operations	5 yr. Retail Sales CAGR% (Local Currency)	5 yr. Net Income CAGR% (Local Currency)
62	US	Kohl's	9,120	9,120	643	US	24.4%	35.5%
63	Japan	Seiyu	9,289	8,811	(740)	Hong Kong SAR, Japan, Singapore, Vietnam	-1.1%	NM
64	UK	Dixons	8,975	8,604	359	Czech Rep., Denmark, Finland, France, Hungary, Iceland, Rep. Of Ireland, Italy, Norway, Spain, Sweden, UK	15.5%	6.7%
65	Italy	COOP Italia	8,560 e	8,560 e	n/a	Croatia, Italy	7.2%	n/a
66	US	Limited Brands	8,445	8,445	528	US	-1.7%	19.5%
67	US	Staples	11,596	8,200 e	446	Canada, Germany, Netherlands, Portugal, UK, US	9.6%	27.8%
68	Switzerland	Coop Switzerland	8,851	8,054	214	Switzerland	0.9%	n/a
69	US	Dell	35,404	8,000 e	2,122	Global	25.9%	17.6%
70	Japan	Takashimaya	9,652	7,949	32	Australia, France, Italy, Japan, Singapore, Taiwan, US	-1.4%	-13.8%
71	US	Dillard's	7,911	7,911	(398)	US	3.6%	NM
72	Sweden	Coop Norden	7,990	7,798	21	Denmark, Norway, Sweden	n/a	n/a
73	US	Office Depot	11,357 e	7,450	311	Austria, Belgium, Canada, Costa Rica, France, Germany, Guatemala, Hungary, Rep. of Ireland, Israel, Italy, Japan, Luxembourg, Mexico, Netherlands, Poland, Portugal, Spain, Switzerland, Thailand, UK, US.	2.1%	14.2%

DT Rank 2003	Country of Origin	Name of Company	Formats	2002 Group Sales* (US$mil) e = estimate	2002 Retail sales (US$mil) e = estimate	2002 Group Income/ (Loss)* (US $mil)	Countries of Operations	5 yr. Retail Sales CAGR% (Local Currency)	5 yr. Net Income CAGR% (Local Currency)
74	Japan	Mitsukoshi	Department	7,680	7,309	51	China, France, Germany, Hong Kong, Italy, Japan, Spain, Taiwan, UK, US	-1.6%	NM
75	UK	Somerfield	Convenience, Discount, Supermarket	7,273	7,273	62	UK	6.0%	NM
76	US	Yum! Brands	Food Service	7,757	6,891	583	Global	-6.0%	NM
77	US	Army & Air Force Exchange Services	Specialty	6,800 e	6,800 e	373	Global	-1.2%	2.1%
78	Canada	Empire/Sobeys	Convenience, Discount, Drug, Supermarket, Superstore	6,772	6,772	116	Canada	27.0%	15.3%
79	UK	Boots	Drug, Specialty	8,242	6,686	468	Hong Kong SAR, Rep. of Ireland, Taiwan, Thailand, UK	-0.1%	-4.8%
80	UK	The Big Food Group	Cash & Carry, Supermarket	7,830	6,639	19	Rep. of Ireland, UK	22.3%	-14.3%
81	S. Korea	Lotte Shopping	Convenience, Department, Food Service, Hypermarket, Supermarket	6,575	6,575	242	China, S. Korea	35.3%	71.5%
82	Japan	Yamada Denki	Specialty	6,517	6,517	46	Japan	37.0%	27.9%
83	UK	Wm Morrison	Supermarket, Superstore	6,514	6,514	276	UK	13.5%	13.9%
84	UK	John Lewis	Department, Hypermarket, Supermarket	6,450	6,450	62	UK	4.2%	-30.3%
85	France	Systeme U	Supermarket, Superstore	6,338 e	6,338 e	n/a	France, Mauritius	10.2%	n/a
86	US	Avon	Direct Selling	6,171	6,171	535	Global	4.0%	9.5%
87	US	Dollar General	Discount	6,100	6,100	265	US	18.4%	12.8%
88	UK	Compass	Food Service	15,620	6,092	672	Australia, Austria, Belgium, Brazil, Canada, France, Germany, Rep. Of Ireland, Japan, Netherlands, Norway, Portugal, Spain, S. Africa, Sweden, Switzerland, UK, US	14.3%	35.1%

DT Rank 2003	Country of Origin	Name of Company	Formats	2002 Group Sales* (US$mil) e = estimate	2002 Retail sales (US$mil) e = estimate	2002 Group Income/(Loss)* (US $mil)	Countries of Operations	5 yr. Retail Sales CAGR% (Local Currency)	5 yr. Net Income CAGR% (Local Currency)
89	US	Nordstrom	Department, Mail Order, Specialty	5,975	5,975	90	US	4.3%	-13.5%
90	US	Saks, Inc.	Department, Specialty	5,911	5,911	24	US	10.8%	-17.6%
91	US	United Auto Group	Auto	7,435 e	5,907 e	62	Brazil, UK, US	n/a	n/a
92	US	BJ's Wholesale Club	Warehouse	5,729	5,729	131	US	14.8%	19.4%
93	US	Sonic Automotive	Auto	7,071 e	5,488 e	107	US	n/a	n/a
94	Japan	Daimaru	Department, Supermarket	6,470	5,449	42	Japan	-2.8%	30.2%
95	Sweden	Hennes & Mauritz	Specialty	5,428	5,428	632	Austria, Belgium, Denmark, Finland, France, Germany, Luxembourg, Netherlands, Norway, Spain, Sweden, Switzerland, UK, US	20.2%	27.5%
96	S Africa	Metcash	Cash & Carry Convenience, Specialty, Supermarket	5,430 e	5,403 e	76	Angola, Australia, Botswana, China, Israel, Kenya, Madagascar, Malawi, Mozambique, New Zealand, South Africa, Uganda, Zambia, Zimbabwe	36.4%	32.1%
97	US	AutoZone	Specialty	5,326	5,326	428	Mexico, US	14.6%	17.0%
98	US	Barnes & Noble	Specialty	5,269	5,269	100	US	13.5%	13.5%
99	US	Menard	DIY	5,250 e	5,250 e	n/a	US	5.6%	n/a
100	Finland	S Group	Convenience, Department, Food Service, Hypermarket, Specialty, Supermarket	6,422 e	5,246 e	42	Estonia, Finland	2.6%	n/a
101	France	Galeries Lafayette	Department, Hypermarket, Mail Order	5,172	5,172	79	France, Germany?	6.4%	-3.2%
102	Germany	Schlecker	Drug, DIY, Hypermarket	5,108 e	5,108 e	n/a	Austria, France, Germany, Italy, Luxembourg, Netherlands, Spain	7.0%	n/a
103	US	CompUSA	Mail Order, Specialty	5,100 e	5,100 e	n/a	US	-0.7%	n/a
104	Spain	Mercadona	Supermarket	5,087	5,087	86	Spain	27.3%	30.5%

DT Rank 2003	Country of Origin	Name of Company	Formats	2002 Group Sales* (US$mil) e = estimate	2002 Retail sales (US$mil) e = estimate	2002 Group Income/(Loss)* (US $mil)	Countries of Operations	5 yr. Retail Sales CAGR% (Local Currency)	5 yr. Net Income CAGR% (Local Currency)
105	S. Korea	Shinsegae	Department, Food Service, Hypermarket	5,049	5,049	199	China, S. Korea	31.9%	89.8%
106	US	DeCA (Defense Commissary Agency)	Commissary	4,963 e	4,963 e	n/a	Azores, Belgium, Egypt, Germany, Guam, Iceland, Italy, Japan, S. Korea, Netherlands, Okinawa, Puerto Rico, Saudi Arabia, Spain, Turkey, UK, US	-0.3%	n/a
107	Austria	SPAR Austria Group	Convenience, Hypermarket, Specialty, Supermarket, Superstore	4,956 e	4,956 e	n/a	Austria, Czech Rep., Hungary, Italy, Slovenia	11.2%	n/a
108	Finland	Kesko	Department, DIY, Discount, Hypermarket, Supermarket, Food Service, Specialty	6,116	4,911	64	Estonia, Finland, Latvia, Lithuania, Sweden	6.5%	-5.1%
109	Japan	Isetan	Department, Specialty, Supermarket	4,942	4,833 e	63	Austria, China, Hong Kong, Italy, Japan, Malaysia, Singapore, Spain, Taiwan, Thailand, US	2.0%	24.6%
110	UK	Cooperative Group	Convenience, Department, Hypermarket, Specialty, Supermarket, Superstore	11,421 e	4,785 e	n/a	UK	11.0%	n/a
111	Norway	NorgesGruppen	Convenience, Discount, Supermarket	5,262 e	4,743 e	n/a	Norway	n/a	n/a
112	Belgium	C&A	Specialty	4,730 e	4,730 e	n/a	Austria, Belgium, Czech Rep., France, Germany, Hungary, Luxembourg, Netherlands, Poland, Portugal, Spain, Switzerland	9.2%	n/a
113	Canada	Hudson's Bay Company	Department, Specialty	4,720	4,669	71	Canada	2.5%	NM
114	US	Darden Restaurants	Food Service	4,655	4,655	232	Canada, US	8.0%	NM
115	US	Radio Shack	Specialty	4,577	4,577	263	Puerto Rico, US, Virgin Islands	-3.2%	7.1%
116	Italy	Conad	Convenience, Hypermarket, Supermarket	4,566 e	4,566 e	263	Italy	3.7%	n/a

DT Rank 2003	Country of Origin	Name of Company	Formats	2002 Group Sales* (US$mil) (e = estimate)	2002 Retail sales (US$mil) (e = estimate)	2002 Group Income/(Loss)* (US $mil)	Countries of Operations	5 yr. Retail Sales CAGR% (Local Currency)	5 yr. Net Income CAGR% (Local Currency)
117	US	Officemax	Mail Order, Specialty	4,776	4,532	74	Mexico, Puerto Rico, US, Virgin Islands	3.8%	-3.9%
118	US	Foot Locker	Mail Order, Specialty	4,509	4,509	144	Australia, Austria, Belgium, Canada, Denmark, France, Germany, Guam, Italy, Rep. of Ireland, Luxembourg, Netherlands, Puerto Rico, Spain, Sweden, UK, US, Virgin Islands	-0.4%	NM
119	Netherlands	VendexKBB	Department, DIY, Specialty	4,533	4,496	194	Belgium, Denmark, France, Germany, Luxembourg, Netherlands	2.5%	-17.2%
120	US	Longs Drugs	Drug	4,426	4,426	7	US	8.4%	-34.5%
121	US	Giant Eagle	Supermarket	5,100 e	4,400	n/a	US	12.4%	n/a
122	US	Alticor/Amway	Direct Selling, e-commerce	4,500 e	4,400 e	n/a	Global	12.2%	n/a
123	Japan	Seibu Department	Department	4,396	4,396	(2,020)	Japan	-3.0%	NM
124	US	Comcast / QVC	TV Shopping	12,460	4,381	(274)	Germany, Japan, UK, US	-0.4%	NM
125	Denmark	Dansk Supermarked	Department, Discount, Hypermarket, Specialty, Superstore	4,344 e	4,344 e	n/a	Denmark, Germany, Poland, Sweden, UK	5.4%	n/a
126	Spain	Eroski	Convenience, Discount, Hypermarket, Specialty, Supermarket, Superstore	4,497	4,326	86	Spain	4.6%	26.0%
127	US	V.T.Inc	Auto	5,436 e	4,250 e	n/a	US	n/a	n/a
128	US	Hy-Vee	Supermarket	4,200 e	4,200 e	n/a	US	7.7%	n/a
129	Japan	Yodobashi Camera	Specialty	4,169	4,169	52	Japan	16.4%	n/a
130	US	Family Dollar	Discount	4,164	4,164	217	US	15.9%	23.7%
131	Japan	Kojima	Specialty	4,133	4,133	2	Japan	10.8%	-31.6%
132	UK	Woolworths (UK)	Department, Specialty	4,128	4,128	52	UK	n/a	n/a
133	US	Pathmark	Supermarket	3,938	3,938	13	US	1.3%	NM

DT Rank 2003	Country of Origin	Name of Company	Formats	2002 Group Sales* (US$mil) e = estimate	2002 Retail sales (US$mil) e = estimate	2002 Group Income/ (Loss)* (US$mil)	Countries of Operations	5 yr. Retail Sales CAGR% (Local Currency)	5 yr. Net Income CAGR% (Local Currency)
134	US	Amazon.com	E-commerce	3,933	3,933	(149)	UK, Germany, Japan, France	92.8%	NM
135	US	Big Lots	Discount	3,869	3,869	77	US	-0.9%	-2.2%
136	France	LeRoy Merlin	DIY, Specialty	3,867	3,867	n/a	Brazil, France, Italy, Poland, Portugal, Spain, China	12.3%	n/a
137	US	Asbury Automotive	Auto	4,469 e	3,863 e	38	US	n/a	n/a
138	US	Bed Bath and Beyond	Specialty	3,665	3,665	302	US	28.0%	32.8%
139	Japan	Marui	Department	4,516	3,588	142	Japan	-1.1%	-1.7%
140	Spain	Inditex	Specialty	3,819	3,585	421	Andorra, Austria, Argentina, Bahrain, Belgium, Brazil, Canada, Chile, Czech Rep., Denmark, Dominican Rep., El Salvador, Finland, France, Germany, Greece, Iceland, Rep. Of Ireland, Israel, Italy, Japan, Jordan, Kuwait, Lebanon, Luxembourg, Mexico, Netherlands, Norway, Poland, Portugal, Puerto Rico, Qatar, Saudi Arabia, Singapore, Spain, Sweden, Switzerland, Turkey, UAE, UK, US, Uruguay, Venezuela	25.1%	30.1%
141	Germany	Globus	DIY, Hypermarket, Specialty	3,569 e	3,569 e	n/a	Czech Rep. Germany	5.0%	n/a
142	US	Ross Stores	Discount Specialty	3,531	3,531	201	US	12.2%	11.4%
143	US	Borders	Specialty	3,513	3,513	112	Australia, New Zealand, Puerto Rico, Singapore, UK, US	9.2%	7.0%
144	US	Group 1 Automotive	Auto	4,011 e	3,448 e	67	US	n/a	n/a
145	Brazil	Pao de Acucar	Discount, Hypermarket, Specialty, Supermarket	3,413	3,413	88	Brazil	24.9%	11.4%
146	Hong Kong	Dairy Farm International	Convenience, Discount, DIY, Drug, Food Service, Hypermarket, Specialty, Supermarket	3,354	3,354	343	China, Hong Kong SAR, India, Indonesia, S. Korea, Malaysia, Singapore, Taiwan	-13.4%	21.6%

DT Rank 2003	Country of Origin	Name of Company	Formats	2002 Group Sales* (US$mil) e = estimate	2002 Retail sales (US$mil) e = estimate	2002 Group Income/(Loss)* (US $mil)	Countries of Operations	5 yr. Retail Sales CAGR% (Local Currency)	5 yr. Net Income CAGR% (Local Currency)
147	UK	Next	Specialty	3,346	3,346	320	UK	13.4%	9.0%
148	Portugal	Sonae/Modelo Continente	Cash & Carry, Convenience, DIY, Hypermarket, Specialty, Supermarket, Superstore	3,346	3,346	95	Brazil, Portugal, Spain	8.2%	6.4%
149	Mexico	Soriana	Hypermarket, Warehouse	3,336	3,336	161	Mexico	13.6%	1.8%
150	Mexico	Controladora Comercial Mexicana	Food Service, Hypermarket, Supermarket, Superstore, Warehouse	3,329	3,329	82	Mexico	12.3%	2.1%
151	US	Sherwin-Williams	Specialty	5,185	3,302	399	Canada, Chile, Brazil, Mexico, Puerto Rico, US, Uruguay, Virgin Islands	4.9%	8.9%
152	US	Advance Auto Parts	Auto	3,288	3,288	65	Puerto Rico, UK, Virgin Islands	23.2%	25.4%
153	Canada	Metro (Metro-Richelieu)	Convenience, Drug, Supermarket, Superstore	3,274	3,274	92	Canada	7.1%	2.1%
154	US	Shopko	Discount	3,253	3,253	(145)	US	5.9%	NM
155	Norway	Reitan	Convenience, Discount, Food Service, Specialty, Supermarket	3,246	3,246	69	Denmark, Estonia, Latvia, Lithuania, Norway, Poland, Slovakia, Sweden	18.0%	n/a
156	Mexico	Grupo Gigante	Discount, Food Service, Specialty, Supermarket, Superstore, Warehouse	3,207	3,207	36	Mexico, US	13.0%	-9.2%
157	US	Raley's	Supermarket	3,200 e	3,200	n/a	US	5.9%	n/a

DT Rank 2003	Country of Origin	Name of Company	Formats	2002 Group Sales* (US$mil) e = estimate	2002 Retail sales (US$mil) e = estimate	2002 Group Income/(Loss)* (US$mil)	Countries of Operations	5 yr. Retail Sales CAGR% (Local Currency)	5 yr. Net Income CAGR% (Local Currency)
158	France	LVMH	Department, Specialty, Supermarket	12,006	3,156	526	Argentina, Australia, Austria, Belgium, Brazil, Canada, Chile, China, Colombia, Czech Republic, Denmark, France, Germany, Greece, Guam, Hong Kong SAR, India, Indonesia, Rep. of Ireland, Israel, Italy, Japan, Korea, Kuwait, Luxembourg, Macao, Malaysia, Mexico, Monaco, Morocco, Netherlands, New Zealand, Philippines, Poland, Portugal, Puerto Rico, Russia, Saipan, Saudi Arabia, Singapore, Spain, Sweden, Switzerland, Taiwan, Thailand, Turkey, UAE, Uruguay, UK, US, Venezuela, Vietnam	8.3%	-4.9%
159	US	Wegman's	Supermarket	3,100 e	3,100 e	n/a	US	5.7%	n/a
160	Japan	Hankyu Department Stores	Department, Supermarket	3,243	3,082	70	Japan	-1.2%	49.2%
161	Japan	Skylark	Food Service	3,069	3,054	(9)	Japan, S. Korea, Taiwan, Thailand, US	6.7%	NM
162	Japan	Izumi	Specialty, Superstore	3,122	3,043	46	Japan	7.8%	33.6%
163	Japan	Matsuzakaya	Department, Supermarket	3,130	3,007	40	France, Japan	-5.3%	NM
164	Canada	Canadian Tire	Convenience, Specialty	3,788	3,003	129	Canada	8.2%	6.3%
165	Japan	Life	Supermarket	3,067	2,990	16	Japan	5.0%	24.7%
166	Japan	Maruetsu	Supermarket	3,023	2,970	10	Japan	2.9%	-3.9%
167	S. Africa	Pick 'n Pay Stores	Convenience, Drug, Hypermarket, Specialty, Supermarket	2,950 e	2,950	51	Australia, Botswana, Namibia, S. Africa, Swaziland, Zimbabwe	19.0%	32.8%
168	Italy	Esselunga	Supermarket	2,948 e	2,948	n/a	Italy	10.1%	n/a
169	Belgium	Colruyt	Cash & Carry, Convenience, Discount, Specialty, Supermarket	3,123	2,942	133	Belgium, France	9.4%	15.6%

DT Rank 2003	Country of Origin	Name of Company	Formats	2002 Group Sales* (US$mil) e = estimate	2002 Retail sales (US$mil) e = estimate	2002 Group Income/ (Loss)* (US $mil)	Countries of Operations	5 yr. Retail Sales CAGR% (Local Currency)	5 yr. Net Income CAGR% (Local Currency)
170	Hong Kong	Hutchison Whampoa/AS Watson	Drug, Specialty, Supermarket	9,647	2,938 e	1,832	Belgium, China, Czech Rep., Hong Kong SAR, Hungary, Luxembourg, Macau, Malaysia, Netherlands, Poland, Philippines, Singapore, Switzerland, Taiwan, Thailand, UK	15.0%	3.1%
171	Germany	Bertelsmann	Mail Order, E-commerce	17,321	2,922	878	Austria, Australia, Belgium, Canada, China, Denmark, Germany, Finland, France, Hungary, Italy, Japan, Netherlands, Poland, Portugal, Sweden, Switzerland, Spain, South Korea, UK, US	6.9%	12.2%
172	UK	Arcadia Group	Mail Order, Specialty	2,900 e	2,900 e	n/a	Austria, Bahrain, Chile, Croatia, Cyprus, Denmark, France, Germany, Hong Kong SAR, Hungary, Iceland, Japan, Kuwait, Lebanon, Malta, Poland, Portugal, Qatar, Rep. of Ireland, Saudi Arabia, Singapore, Slovenia, Spain, Taiwan, Turkey, UAE, UK, US	-2.4%	n/a
173	US	Payless ShoeSource	Specialty	2,878	2,878	106	Canada, Guam, Puerto Rico, Saipan, US, Virgin Islands	2.3%	-3.9%
174	US	Neiman Marcus	Mail Order, Specialty	2,948	2,877	100	US	5.4%	1.6%
175	US	Michaels Stores, Inc.	Specialty	2,856	2,856	140	Canada, US	14.4%	36.1%
176	Netherlands	SHV Makro	Cash & Carry	2,831 e	2,831 e	n/a	Argentina, Brazil, China, Colombia, Indonesia, Malaysia, Philippines, Taiwan, Thailand, Venezuela	1.3%	n/a
177	S. Africa	Shoprite Holdings	Cash & Carry, Convenience, Discount, Food Service, Hypermarket, Specialty, Supermarket	2,812	2,812	47	Botswana, Egypt, Lesotho, Madagascar, Malawi, Mozambique, Namibia, Swaziland, South Africa, Tanzania, Zambia, Zimbabwe	11.4%	11.7%
178	Japan	Tokyu Department Store	Department	3,481	2,808	92	Japan	-1.8%	-5.9%

DT Rank 2003	Country of Origin	Name of Company	Formats	e = estimate	2002 Group Sales* (US$mil)	e = estimate	2002 Retail sales (US$mil)	2002 Group Income/(Loss)* (US$mil)	Countries of Operations	5 yr. Retail Sales CAGR% (Local Currency)	5 yr. Net Income CAGR% (Local Currency)
179	US	Starbucks	Food Service		3,289		2,793	215	Australia, Austria, Bahrain, Canada, China, Germany, Greece, Indonesia, Israel, Japan, Kuwait, Lebanon, Malaysia, Mexico, New Zealand, Oman, Philippines, Puerto Rico, Qatar, Saudi Arabia, Singapore, S. Korea, Spain, Switzerland, Taiwan, Thailand, UAE, UK, US	27.5%	31.4%
180	UK	Littlewoods	Department, Mail Order	e	2,752	e	2,752	n/a	UK	-9.6%	n/a
181	Japan	Izumiya	Specialty, Supermarket, Superstore		2,801		2,729	17	Japan	-3.4%	-10.8%
182	Japan	Heiwado	Specialty, Supermarket, Superstore		2,858		2,721	39	China, Japan	4.1%	23.8%
183	Japan	Fast Retailing	Specialty		2,753		2,713	223	China, Japan, UK	35.2%	59.4%
184	US	Burlington Coat Factory	Specialty		2,697		2,697	65	US	8.7%	3.0%
185	US	PETsMART	Specialty		2,695		2,695	89	Canada, US	8.5%	NM
186	US	Whole Foods Markets	Hypermarket		2,691		2,691	85	Canada, US	20.7%	26.2%
187	Japan	Kintetsu Department	Department, Supermarket		3,453		2,670	13	Japan	1.4%	-64.8%
188	US	Stater Bros.	Supermarket		2,666		2,666	12	US	10.1%	n/a
189	Canada	Jean Coutu	Drug		2,661		2,661	108	Canada, US	15.9%	21.1%
190	US	Spiegel	Mail Order, Specialty	e	2,650	e	2,650	n/a	US, Canada	-1.3%	n/a
191	Canada	Shoppers Drug Mart	Drug		2,561		2,561	133	Canada	0.0%	5.6%
192	US	The Pantry	Convenience		2,495		2,495	2	US	42.3%	NM
193	Germany	Dohle	Cash & Carry, Department, Discount, DIY, Hypermarket, Specialty, Supermarket, Superstore	e	2,587	e	2,489	n/a	Germany	0.4%	n/a

DT Rank 2003	Country of Origin	Name of Company	Formats	2002 Group Sales* (US$mil) e = estimate	2002 Retail sales (US$mil) e = estimate	2002 Group Income/ (Loss)* (US$mil)	Countries of Operations	5 yr. Retail Sales CAGR% (Local Currency)	5 yr. Net Income CAGR% (Local Currency)
194	UK	Debenhams	Department	2,472	2,472	160	Bahrain, Dubai, Hungary, Kuwait, Rep. of Ireland, UK	5.6%	6.3%
195	US	Price Chopper	Superstore	2,470 e	2,470 e	n/a	US	3.9%	n/a
196	US	Value City	Department, Specialty	2,451	2,451	(4)	US	17.9%	NM
197	Australia	Foodland	Cash & Carry, Convenience, Department, Specialty, Supermarket	2,439	2,439	54	Australia, New Zealand	4.3%	9.4%
198	Japan	Best Denki	Specialty	2,890	2,417	(9)	Hong Kong, Japan, Malaysia, Singapore	12.3%	NM
199	US	Charming Shoppes	Specialty	2,412	2,412	(3)	US	18.9%	NM
200	Germany	dm	Drug	2,401 e	2,401 e	n/a	Austria, Croatia, Czech Rep., Germany, Hungary, Italy, Slovakia, Slovenia	16.9%	n/a

* includes non-retail
n/a = not available
NM = not meaningful
e = estimate
CAGR = Compound Annual Growth Rate
Name after forward slash is retail segment of parent company

Data prepared with assistance from M+M Planet Retail, UK. Five-year growth rates were computed using the latest local currency figures and the 1997 results contained in the February 1999 Global Powers of Retailing. For retailers not on that earlier list, data were taken from annual reports.

Source: Reprinted courtesy of Deloitte Touche Tohmatsu from Stores, January 2004, National Retail Foederation.

Appendix B:

Rethinking the Regional Shopping Center Layout

Rethinking the Regional Shopping Center Layout

NON-STRATEGIC CENTER LAYOUT

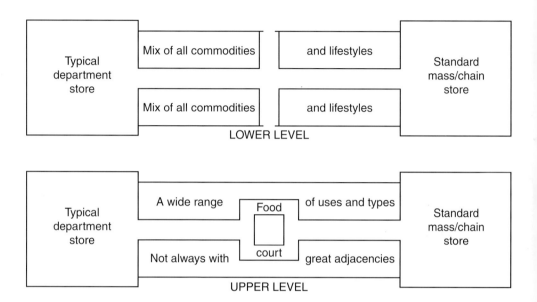

STORES CLUSTERED TO CREATE SPECIAL LIFESTYLE NEIGHBORHOODS

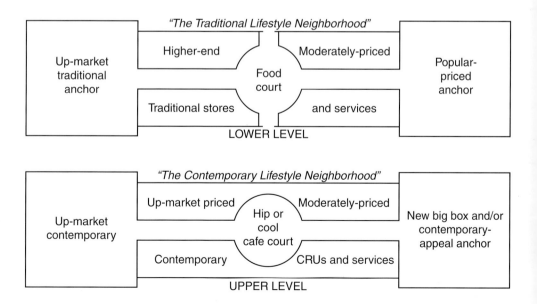

Resources

American Marketing Association

311 South Wacker Drive, Chicago, Illinois 60606

(800) AMA-1150

(312) 542-9000

www.marketingpower.com

Direct Marketing Association

1120 Avenue of the Americas, New York, New York 10036-6700

(212) 768-7277

www.the-dma.org

Institute of Store Planners

25 North Broadway, Tarrytown, New York 10591

(914) 332-1806

www.ispo.org

International Association of Business Communicators (IABC)

One Hallidie Plaza, Suite 600, San Francisco, California 94102

(415) 544-4700

www.iabc.com

International Council of Shopping Centers

1221 Avenue of the Americas, New York, New York 10020-1099

(646) 728-3800

www.icsc.org

Marketing Research Association

1344 Silas Deane Hwy., Suite 306, Rocky Hills, CT 06067-0230

(860) 257-4008

www.mra-net.org

National Association of Visual Merchandisers

13304 Rainbow One, Suite 201, Austin, Texas 78734

(512) 266-0224

www.visualmerch.com

National Retail Federation (NRF)

325 7th Street North West, Suite 1100, Washington, DC 20004

(800) 673-4692

www.nrf.com

Point of Purchase Advertising Institute

1660 L. Street North West, 10th Floor, Washington, DC 20036

(202) 530-3000

www.popai.com

Retail Advertising and Marketing Association

325 7th Street North West, Suite 1100, Washington, DC 20004

(202) 662-3052

www.rama-nrf.org

Retail Council of Canada

1255 Bay Street, Suite 800, Toronto, Ontario, Canada M5R 2A9

(416) 922-6678

www.retailcouncil.com

There are also many state- and provincial-based retail
organizations that can be a resource.

Periodicals and
Online
Newsletters

Advertising Age

Includes news and features related to advertising and marketing in
the US and overseas.

Crain Communications, Inc., 1400 Woodbridge Avenue, New York,
New York 10017

(212) 210-0100

www.aamedia.chaffee.com

American Demographics

Business magazine of demographic trends, sources, and techniques.

c/o Customer Service, P.O. Box 2042, Marion, Ohio 43306-8142

(800) 329-7502

www.demographics.ca

Chain Store Age

Merchandise information, operating techniques, training material, ad
industry news for headquarters executives and store managers.

Lebhar-Friedman, 425 Park Avenue, New York, New York 10022

(212) 371-9400

www.chainstoreage.com

Discount Store News

Information on planning, merchandising, and operating discount
stores. Spot news and feature reports on developments in the
discount store field.

Lebhar-Friedman, 425 Park Avenue, New York, New York 10022

(212) 371-9400

www.discountstorenews.com

Mark McCormack's Success Secrets

Offers techniques for improving managerial skills and performance.

1360 East 9th Street, Suite 100, Cleveland, Ohio 44114

(216) 436-3431

www.successsecrets.com

Marketing News

Current articles on marketing and association activities.

311 South Wacker Drive, Chicago, Illinois 60606

(800) AMA-1150

(312) 542-9000

www.marketingpower.com

Men's Ad Review

Ideas for advertising by specialty types; includes recent effective ads in bimonthly bulletin.

Retail Reporting Corporation, 101 Fifth Avenue, New York, NY 10001

(212) 255-9595

National Retail Bulletin United States and Canada

Information and insights on the retail sales numbers released in both the United States and Canada.

USA

J.C. Williams Group

350 West Hubbard Street, Suite 240, Chicago, Illinois 60610

(312) 673-1254

www.jcwg.com

Canada

J.C. Williams Group

17 Dundonald Street, 3rd Floor, Toronto, Ontario, Canada M4Y 1K3

(416) 921-4181

www.jcwg.com

NRF Smartbrief

Daily updates on the most recent retail news.

National Retail Federation, 325 7th Street North West, Suite 1100,

Washington, DC 20004

(800) 673-4692

www.nrf.com

Retail Ad World

Depicts the best creative that leading retailers, manufacturers, catalog
companies, shopping centers and e-tailers are doing to enhance their
image, build customer relationships and attract customers.

Visual Reference Publications, Inc., 302 Fifth Avenue, New York,

New York 10001

(800) 251-4545 (U.S. and Canada)

www.retailreporting.com

Retail Design and Visual Presentation

Provides information on the latest trends in new materials, fixturing,
lighting, interior design, visual merchandising and store layout,
displays, props, signage, and more.

Visual Reference Publications, Inc., 302 Fifth Avenue, New York,

New York 10001

(800) 251-4545 (U.S. and Canada)

www.retailreporting.com

The Retail Challenge

Provides helpful tips and strategies for retailers.

ICSC, 1221 Avenue of the Americas

New York, NY 10020-1099

(646) 728-3800

www.icsc.org

Retail Forward

Provides latest retail news.

700 Ackerman Place, Suite 600, Columbus, Ohio 43202

Phone: (614) 355-4000

www.retailforward.com

Sales and Marketing Management

Directed at executives responsible for managing sales and marketing functions in their organizations.

Billboard Communications, 633 Third Avenue, New York, NY 10017

(800) 562-2706

(818) 487-4582

www.salesandmarketing.com

Shop.org

Weekly update on online retail.

325 7th Street, NW, Suite 1100, Washington, DC 20004

(202) 626-8190

www.shop.org

Signs of the Times

The sign field, including electric, illuminated signs, and outdoor advertising.

407 Gilbert Avenue, Cincinnati, Ohio 45202

(513) 421-2050

www.stmediagroup.com

Stores

For retail executives whose responsibilities include areas of merchandising and financing, delineates and interprets strategies and tactics.

325 7th Street North West, Suite 1100, Washington, DC 20004

(800) 673-4692

www.nrf.com

Value Retail News

The place to go for the latest news and trends in value retailing.

ICSC, 1221 Avenue of the Americas

New York, NY 10020-1099

(646) 728-3800

www.icsc.org

Visual Merchandising and Store Design

Highlights new products, trends and useful statistics, pointing the way to more profitable retailing and merchandising.

Signs of the Times Publications

407 Gilbert Avenue, Cincinnati, OH 45202

(513) 421-2050

www.visualstore.ca

Women's Wear Daily

Retail trade publication covering women's and children's apparel,
accessories, and cosmetics.

Fairchild Publications, 7 East 12th Street, New York, New York 10003

(212) 741-4000

www.wwd.com

Internet Sources

Bureau of Labor Statistics

Office, other

www.stats.bls.gov

CBS MarketWatch – Market Data

Retail, industrial

www.cbs.marketwatch.com

Claritas

Population estimates

www.claritas.com

Colliers International Market

Office, residential, industrial

www.collier.com

The Conference Board of Canada

Conferences, events

www.conferenceboard.ca

Hospitality Net

Events, hospitality

www.hospitalitynet.org

ICSC Research

Government, retail

www.icsc.org

ITA Tourism Industries

Tourism

www.tinet.ita.doc.gov

National Retail Federation

Retail

www.nrf.com

The North American Real Estate Review

Office, Industrial

www.narer.com

Statistics Canada

Office, retail, hospitality, residential, industrial, other

www.statcan.ca

Strategis

Office, retail, events, industrial, other

www.strategic.ic.gc.ca

US Census Bureau

Office, culture, residential, other

www.census.gov

World Tourism Statistics Service

Tourism

www.world-tourism.org

**Retail
Consultants,
Consumer and
Market Research
Specialists**

See ICSC's *Membership and Products & Services Directory.*

About the Author

John C. Williams

Senior Partner

J.C. Williams Group Limited, Chicago and Toronto

www.jcwg.com

Since starting this consulting company in 1974, John Williams has been recognized as one of North America's retail, shopping center, and urban revitalization gurus. During these years, John has consulted to a wide range of clients where his work is known for its creative approach to achieving results. J.C. Williams Group's consultants specialize in retailing, real estate, market research, branding and marketing, multichannel distribution, and information technology for a wide range of leading retail-related businesses.

John has co-authored *A Guide to Retail Success* for the National Retail Federation, Washington D.C., as well as *Building a Winning Retail Strategy* for the Retail Council of Canada, *Retail Revitalization and Recruitment Action Program for Downtowns,* for the International Downtown Association, and now *Getting Retail Right!* for ICSC. He is a frequent speaker at industry and association gatherings across the continent, as well as ICSC's University of Shopping Centers.

John received his Bachelor of Commerce degree from the University of British Columbia, an MBA from the top-ranked Kellogg School of Graduate Management at Northwestern University (www.kellogg.nwu.edu), and has attended postgraduate courses at Harvard.